How to Start a Home Baking Business

Copyright © 2024

All rights reserved. No part of this book may be reproduced in any form or by any electronic or mechanical means, including information storage and retrieval systems, without permission in writing from the publisher, except by a reviewer, who may quote brief passages in a review.

The information contained in this book is for general information purposes only. The information is provided by naciro and while we endeavor to keep the information up to date and correct, we make no representations or warranties of any kind, express or implied, about the completeness, accuracy, reliability, suitability or availability with respect to the book or the information, products, services, or related graphics contained in the book for any purpose. Any reliance you place on such information is therefore strictly at your own risk.

All trademarks and registered trademarks are the property of their respective owners and are used in this book only for identification and explanation.

Permission to use copyrighted material in this book should be obtained from the copyright owner or the publisher.

This book is not intended to provide medical, legal, or financial advice, and the author and publisher specifically disclaim any liability for any loss or damage caused or alleged to be caused directly or indirectly by the information in this book.

Naciro and the publisher of this book do not endorse or recommend any commercial products, processes, or services. The views and opinions of authors expressed in this book do not necessarily state or reflect those of the publisher of this book.

Contents

Chapter 1: Introduction to Home Baking Business

Chapter 2: Finding Your Niche

Chapter 3: Setting Up Your Home Kitchen

Chapter 4: Legal Requirements and Permits

Chapter 5: Creating a Business Plan

Chapter 6: Pricing Your Products and Understanding Profitability

Chapter 7: Marketing Strategies to Promote Your Home Baking Business

Chapter 8 Operational Aspects of Running Your Home Baking Business

Chapter 9: Navigating Legal and Regulatory Requirements

Chapter 10: Financial Management and Bookkeeping Practices

Chapter 11: Marketing Strategies for Your Home Baking Business

Chapter 12: Customer Service Strategies for Your Home Baking Business

Chapter 13: Growth Strategies for Scaling Your Home Baking Business

Chapter 14: Management Strategies for Your Home Baking Business

Chapter 15: Financial Planning Strategies for Your Home Baking Business

Chapter 16: Sustainability Practices for Your Home Baking Business

Chapter 17: Marketing Strategies and Digital Presence for Your Home Baking Business

Chapter 18: Customer Service Excellence for Your Home Baking Business

Chapter 19: Operational Efficiency and Productivity Strategies

Chapter 20: Growth Strategies and Expansion Opportunities

Chapter 21: Legal Considerations, Regulatory Compliance, and Business Ethics

Chapter 22: Marketing Strategies and Promotional Tactics

Chapter 23: Customer Relationship Management (CRM) Strategies

Chapter 24: Operational Resilience and Crisis Management

Chapter 25: Innovation in Product Development and Menu Diversification

Chapter 26: Financial Management and Profitability Analysis

Chapter 27: Marketing Strategies and Branding Initiatives

Chapter 28: Customer Service Excellence and Retention Strategies

Chapter 29: Legal Considerations and Risk Management

Chapter 30: Continuous Improvement, Innovation, and Growth Strategies

Detailed Book Introduction

Starting a home baking business is an exciting venture that allows you to turn your passion for baking into a profitable enterprise. Whether you have always loved creating delicious baked goods for friends and family, or you have recently discovered your talent in the kitchen, a home baking business can offer a fulfilling and flexible career path.

This book, "How to Start a Home Baking Business," is designed to guide you through every step of the process, from the initial idea to a thriving business. With the growing popularity of home-based businesses and the increasing demand for unique, homemade products, there has never been a better time to enter the baking industry.

Why a Home Baking Business?

Home baking businesses have several advantages. First, they require relatively low start-up costs compared to other types of food businesses. You can often use your existing kitchen equipment and gradually invest in more specialized tools as your business grows. Second, operating from home provides flexibility in your schedule, allowing you to balance your business with personal commitments. Additionally, there is a growing consumer trend towards supporting local and small-scale producers, making your home-baked goods highly appealing.

What This Book Covers

This comprehensive guide covers all the essential aspects of starting and running a successful home baking business. Each chapter is packed with practical advice, expert tips, and real-life examples to help you navigate the challenges and make informed decisions.

In the first few chapters, we will explore how to identify your niche and set up your home kitchen for efficient and safe production. You will learn about the legal requirements and permits necessary for operating a home-based food business, ensuring you comply with local regulations.

Creating a solid business plan is crucial for any new venture. We will walk you through the process of writing a business plan that outlines your goals, target market, and financial projections. This plan will serve as a roadmap for your business and help you stay focused on your objectives.

One of the most important aspects of your business will be sourcing high-quality ingredients and reliable equipment. We will provide tips on finding suppliers, managing costs, and maintaining consistent product quality. Pricing your products correctly is also vital to your success, and we will discuss various pricing strategies to ensure you remain competitive while making a profit.

Branding and packaging play a significant role in attracting customers. You will learn how to create a strong brand identity that reflects your unique style and values. Effective marketing strategies, including social media, are essential for reaching a broader audience. We will guide you through setting up and maintaining a social media presence that engages and grows your customer base.

Building a professional website and online store is another critical component of modern business. We will cover the basics of web design, e-commerce platforms, and managing online orders and deliveries. Excellent customer service will help you build a loyal customer base, and we will share tips on how to exceed customer expectations.

As your business grows, you may consider expanding your product line and even moving beyond your home kitchen. We will discuss the logistics of scaling up, hiring staff, and managing increased production. Dealing with competition and staying updated with industry trends are ongoing challenges that we will address, providing strategies to keep your business relevant and competitive.

Finally, we will delve into the importance of financial management, networking, participating in local markets, and maintaining health and safety standards in your kitchen. Sustainability and eco-friendly practices are becoming increasingly important to consumers, and we will explore ways to incorporate these principles into your business.

Conclusion

Starting a home baking business is a rewarding journey that combines creativity, entrepreneurship, and the joy of sharing your culinary talents with others. This book is your comprehensive guide to navigating this journey successfully. Whether you are a seasoned baker or a newcomer to the world of business, the knowledge and insights shared in these pages will equip you with the tools you need to build a thriving home baking business. Let's embark on this delicious adventure together!

Chapter 1: Introduction to Home Baking Business

The aroma of freshly baked bread, the sight of perfectly frosted cupcakes, and the satisfaction of creating delicious treats from scratch—these are just a few of the joys of baking. For many, baking is not just a hobby but a passion, a form of creative expression, and a way to bring joy to others. If you have ever dreamed of turning this passion into a profitable business, then starting a home baking business might be the perfect path for you.

Why Start a Home Baking Business?

There are several compelling reasons to start a home baking business. First and foremost, it allows you to do what you love while earning an income. Unlike traditional brick-and-mortar businesses, a home baking business requires lower initial investment and operational costs. You already have a kitchen, and you can often start with the equipment you have on hand, expanding your tools and resources as your business grows.

The flexibility of a home baking business is another significant advantage. You can set your own hours, allowing you to balance work with personal commitments. This flexibility is particularly beneficial for parents, caregivers, or anyone looking to supplement their income without committing to a full-time job outside the home.

Moreover, there is a growing market for homemade, artisanal products. Consumers are increasingly interested in supporting local businesses and purchasing high-quality, unique baked goods that they cannot find in commercial bakeries. Your home baking business can cater to this demand, offering personalized and distinctive products that stand out in the market.

The Essentials of Starting a Home Baking Business

Before you dive into the world of home baking business, it is important to understand the basics. Starting a business, even from home, requires careful planning and preparation. Here are some essential steps to get you started:

1. **Identify Your Niche**

The first step in starting your home baking business is to identify your niche. What type of baked goods are you passionate about and skilled at making? Do you specialize in bread, pastries, cakes, cookies, or a specific type of dessert? Identifying your niche will help you focus your efforts and build a brand around your unique offerings.

Consider conducting market research to understand what types of baked goods are in demand in your area. Look at what local bakeries and home bakers are offering and identify gaps in the market that you can fill. Your niche might also be influenced by dietary trends, such as gluten-free, vegan, or low-sugar options, which are becoming increasingly popular.

2. **Set Up Your Home Kitchen**

Your kitchen is the heart of your baking business, and it needs to be set up efficiently to ensure smooth operations. Start by organizing your workspace to maximize productivity and minimize clutter. Invest in essential baking equipment such as mixers, ovens, baking sheets, and utensils. Depending on your niche, you might also need specialized tools such as cake decorating supplies, bread proofing baskets, or pastry cutters.

Ensure that your kitchen meets health and safety standards required for food businesses. This might involve upgrading your appliances, improving ventilation, or implementing strict hygiene practices. Some regions also require home kitchens to pass health inspections before they can be used for commercial purposes.

3. **Understand the Legal Requirements**

Operating a home baking business comes with legal responsibilities. You need to comply with local regulations and obtain the necessary permits and licenses. These requirements vary depending on your location, so it is essential to research and understand the laws that apply to your business.

Common legal requirements include food handling permits, business licenses, and adherence to health and safety regulations. Some areas have specific cottage food laws that allow the production and sale of certain low-risk foods from home kitchens. Familiarize yourself with these laws and ensure that your business operations are compliant.

4. **Create a Business Plan**

A well-thought-out business plan is the foundation of any successful business. It outlines your goals, target market, competitive analysis, marketing strategies, and financial projections. Writing a business plan helps you clarify your vision and provides a roadmap for achieving your objectives.

Your business plan should include:

- **Executive Summary:** A brief overview of your business, including your mission statement and key objectives.

- **Market Analysis:** Research on your target market, including demographics, preferences, and competition.
- **Business Structure:** Details on your business structure, ownership, and management team.
- **Product Line:** A description of the baked goods you plan to offer, including any unique selling points.
- **Marketing and Sales Strategy:** Your plans for promoting your business and attracting customers.
- **Financial Plan:** Budget, pricing strategy, sales forecasts, and funding requirements.

5. **Source Ingredients and Equipment**

Quality ingredients are the cornerstone of delicious baked goods. Establish relationships with reliable suppliers who can provide you with fresh, high-quality ingredients consistently. Consider sourcing locally whenever possible to support other small businesses and appeal to consumers who prioritize local and sustainable products.

Investing

in the right equipment is equally important. As your business grows, you might need to upgrade your tools to handle increased production. Prioritize equipment that enhances efficiency and ensures consistent product quality.

Building Your Brand and Marketing Your Business

Once you have laid the groundwork for your home baking business, the next step is to build your brand and attract customers. Your brand is more than just your business name and logo; it represents your values, style, and the experience you offer to your customers.

1. **Develop Your Brand Identity**

Create a brand identity that reflects your unique offerings and resonates with your target audience. This includes choosing a business name, designing a logo, and developing a consistent visual style for your packaging, marketing materials, and online presence. Your brand identity should convey the quality, creativity, and personality of your baked goods.

2. **Create a Strong Online Presence**

In today's digital age, having an online presence is crucial for any business. Build a professional website that showcases your products, tells your story, and provides an easy way for customers to place orders. Use high-quality photos and engaging descriptions to highlight the features and benefits of your baked goods.

Leverage social media platforms to connect with your audience, share behind-the-scenes content, and promote your products. Platforms like Instagram and Facebook are particularly effective for showcasing visually appealing baked goods and engaging with potential customers.

3. **Utilize Effective Marketing Strategies**

Marketing your home baking business involves a combination of online and offline strategies. In addition to your online presence, consider participating in local events, farmers markets, and fairs to increase your visibility and reach new customers. Network with local businesses and community organizations to build relationships and create opportunities for collaboration.

Offer promotions, discounts, and special offers to attract new customers and encourage repeat business. Collect customer feedback and use it to improve your products and services continuously.

Conclusion

Starting a home baking business is a rewarding endeavor that allows you to turn your passion into profit. With careful planning, dedication, and a commitment to quality, you can build a successful business that brings joy to your customers and fulfillment to your life. This book will guide you through every step of the process, providing you with the knowledge and tools you need to achieve your entrepreneurial dreams. Let's get started on this delicious journey together!

Chapter 2: Finding Your Niche

Finding your niche is one of the most critical steps in establishing your home baking business. Your niche defines your specialty and sets you apart from the competition. It helps you attract a specific audience and build a loyal customer base. In this chapter, we will explore how to identify and refine your niche, ensuring your business stands out in the market.

Understanding the Importance of a Niche

In the competitive world of baking, having a niche allows you to focus your efforts on creating products that meet the unique needs and preferences of a specific group of customers. This specialization can lead to higher customer satisfaction, repeat business, and word-of-mouth referrals. A well-defined niche also makes your marketing efforts more effective, as you can tailor your messaging and promotions to resonate with your target audience.

Steps to Identify Your Niche

1. **Assess Your Skills and Interests**

Start by evaluating your baking skills and interests. What types of baked goods do you enjoy making the most? Where do your strengths lie? Perhaps you are known for your beautifully decorated cakes, or maybe your friends rave about your delicious cookies. Your niche should align with your passion and expertise, as this will ensure you remain motivated and dedicated to your business.

2. **Conduct Market Research**

Market research is essential to understanding the demand for various types of baked goods in your area. Visit local bakeries, farmers markets, and online platforms to see what products are popular and identify any gaps in the market. Look for trends and consider how you can offer something unique or different.

For example, if you notice a lack of vegan or gluten-free options in your area, this could be an opportunity to fill that gap. Pay attention to customer reviews and feedback to gain insights into what people are looking for and what they feel is missing from the current offerings.

3. **Analyze Your Competition**

Understanding your competition is crucial in finding a niche that sets you apart. Analyze the strengths and weaknesses of other home bakers and commercial bakeries in your area. What are they doing well, and where are they falling short? Identify areas where you can differentiate yourself, whether it's through product quality, unique flavors, exceptional customer service, or innovative packaging.

4. Define Your Unique Selling Proposition (USP)

Your unique selling proposition (USP) is what makes your business stand out from the rest. It's the reason customers will choose your products over those of your competitors. Your USP could be anything from the use of organic ingredients, special dietary options, creative designs, or a unique cultural influence. Clearly define your USP and make it a central part of your branding and marketing efforts.

5. Test Your Ideas

Before committing fully to a niche, it's a good idea to test your ideas on a small scale. Create sample products and seek feedback from friends, family, and potential customers. Participate in local events or farmers markets to gauge interest and gather valuable insights. This testing phase will help you refine your products and confirm that there is a demand for your chosen niche.

Popular Niches in the Baking Industry

To inspire you, here are some popular niches within the baking industry that have proven to be successful:

1. Custom Cakes and Cupcakes

Specializing in custom cakes and cupcakes for events such as weddings, birthdays, and corporate gatherings can be highly lucrative. Customers are willing to pay a premium for beautifully designed and personalized creations that add a special touch to their celebrations.

2. Dietary-Specific Baking

With the increasing awareness of food allergies and dietary preferences, there is a growing demand for gluten-free, vegan, keto, and other specialty baked goods. Catering to these dietary needs can help you attract a dedicated customer base that values your attention to their specific requirements.

3. **Artisanal Bread**

The artisanal bread market has seen a resurgence in recent years, with consumers seeking high-quality, handcrafted loaves made with traditional techniques and natural ingredients. If you have a passion for bread making, this niche can be very rewarding.

4. **Ethnic and Cultural Baked Goods**

Offering baked goods that reflect your cultural heritage or unique ethnic recipes can set you apart from mainstream bakeries. Whether it's Italian biscotti, French pastries, or Middle Eastern sweets, this niche allows you to introduce customers to new and exciting flavors.

5. **Healthy and Organic Options**

Health-conscious consumers are always on the lookout for baked goods made with organic, whole-grain, and low-sugar ingredients. If you can create delicious treats that align with these health trends, you can tap into a market that is willing to pay a premium for quality and nutrition.

6. **Decorative Cookies**

Decorative and themed cookies are popular for parties, holidays, and corporate gifts. If you have a talent for intricate designs and decorations, this niche can be a fun and profitable avenue to explore.

Developing Your Product Line

Once you have identified your niche, the next step is to develop a product line that showcases your specialty. Here are some tips for creating a compelling product line:

1. **Start with a Signature Product**

Begin by perfecting one or two signature products that represent your niche. These products should highlight your unique skills and set the standard for quality in your business. Having a signature product helps establish your reputation and provides a focal point for your marketing efforts.

2. **Expand Gradually**

As your business grows, gradually expand your product line to include complementary items that appeal to your target audience. For example, if your niche is custom cakes, you might add cupcakes, cake pops, and decorated cookies to your offerings. Ensure that each new product maintains the same level of quality and aligns with your brand.

3. **Consider Seasonal and Limited-Edition Items**

Seasonal and limited-edition items can create excitement and encourage repeat purchases. Consider offering special products for holidays, local events, or based on seasonal ingredients. These limited-time offerings can also help you test new ideas without making a long-term commitment.

4. **Gather Customer Feedback**

Regularly seek feedback from your customers to understand their preferences and improve your products. Encourage reviews and suggestions, and be open to making adjustments based on their input.

Customer feedback is invaluable for refining your product line and ensuring it meets the needs of your target market.

Conclusion

Finding your niche is a crucial step in building a successful home baking business. By assessing your skills, conducting market research, analyzing your competition, and defining your unique selling proposition, you can identify a specialty that sets you apart and attracts loyal customers. With a well-defined niche and a carefully curated product line, you are well on your way to establishing a thriving home baking business.

Chapter 3: Setting Up Your Home Kitchen

Your kitchen is the heart of your home baking business, and setting it up efficiently is essential for smooth operations and high-quality production. In this chapter, we will explore how to organize your kitchen, invest in essential equipment, and ensure it meets health and safety standards.

Organizing Your Workspace

An organized kitchen is key to maximizing productivity and minimizing stress. Here are some tips for setting up an efficient workspace:

1. **Designate Specific Areas**

Divide your kitchen into specific areas for different tasks such as mixing, baking, decorating, and packaging. Having designated areas helps streamline your workflow and prevents cross-contamination. For example, keep your mixing and baking station separate from your decorating and packaging area.

2. **Optimize Counter Space**

Counter space is valuable real estate in a baking kitchen. Keep your counters clear and clutter-free by storing ingredients, utensils, and equipment in cabinets and drawers. Use vertical storage solutions such as shelves and hooks to maximize space and keep frequently used items within easy reach.

3. **Use Clear Containers**

Store your ingredients in clear, airtight containers to keep them fresh and easily identifiable. Label each container with the ingredient name and expiration date. This practice not only helps with organization but also ensures you can quickly see when you need to restock.

4. **Invest in a Rolling Cart**

A rolling cart can be a versatile addition to your kitchen, providing extra storage and workspace that can be moved as needed. Use it to store frequently used tools, ingredients, or even as a mobile prep station.

5. **Maintain Cleanliness**

A clean kitchen is essential for food safety and efficiency. Develop a routine for cleaning and sanitizing your workspace, equipment, and utensils. Regularly deep clean your kitchen to prevent the buildup of grime and bacteria. Implement a system for waste disposal and recycling to keep your kitchen tidy.

Essential Baking Equipment

Investing in the right equipment is crucial for producing high-quality baked goods consistently. Here is a list of essential equipment for your home baking business:

1. **Oven**

A reliable oven is the cornerstone of your baking operation. Ensure your oven is capable of maintaining consistent temperatures and can handle the volume of baking you plan to do. If your budget allows, consider investing in a commercial-grade oven for greater capacity and efficiency.

2. **Stand Mixer**

A stand mixer is a versatile and time-saving tool for mixing doughs, batters, and frostings. Choose a model with a powerful motor and various attachments to handle different tasks. A stand mixer can significantly improve your efficiency and ensure consistent results.

3. **Baking Pans and Sheets**

Invest in a variety of high-quality baking pans and sheets, including cake pans, muffin tins, cookie sheets, and loaf pans. Non-stick and heavy-duty options are preferable for even baking and easy cleanup.

4. **Measuring Tools**

Accurate measurements are crucial in baking. Stock up on measuring cups, spoons, and a digital kitchen scale to ensure precision in your recipes. A scale is particularly important for weighing ingredients like flour and sugar, which can vary significantly when measured by volume.

5. **Mixing Bowls and Utensils**

Have a selection of mixing bowls in various sizes, as well as essential utensils such as spatulas, whisks, wooden spoons, and pastry brushes. Silicone spatulas are especially useful for scraping bowls and spreading batter evenly.

6. **Cooling Racks**

Cooling racks are essential for allowing your baked goods to cool evenly and prevent them from becoming soggy. Invest in several sturdy racks to accommodate multiple batches of baking.

7. **Decorating Tools**

If your niche involves decorated cakes, cookies, or pastries, you will need a range of decorating tools. This includes piping bags, tips, offset spatulas, fondant tools, and edible decorations. A turntable can be helpful for decorating cakes.

8. **Storage Containers**

Proper storage is key to maintaining the freshness and quality of your baked goods. Invest in airtight containers for storing finished products, as well as ingredients. Consider using stackable containers to save space.

Ensuring Health and Safety Standards

Compliance with health and safety standards is not only a legal requirement but also essential for producing safe and high-quality baked goods. Here are some guidelines to ensure your kitchen meets these standards:

1. **Food Handling Permits**

Depending on your location, you may need to obtain food handling permits and undergo inspections to operate a home baking business legally. Research the requirements in your area and ensure you comply with all regulations.

2. **Hygiene Practices**

Implement strict hygiene practices in your kitchen. This includes regular handwashing, wearing clean clothing and aprons, and using hairnets or hats to prevent hair contamination. Avoid working when you are ill to prevent the risk of contaminating your products.

3. **Sanitization**

Develop a routine for sanitizing your workspace, equipment, and utensils. Use food-safe sanitizers and follow recommended procedures for cleaning and disinfecting surfaces. Pay special attention to areas where raw ingredients, especially eggs and dairy, are handled.

4. **Pest Control**

Maintain a pest-free kitchen by keeping your workspace clean, storing ingredients in sealed containers, and regularly inspecting for signs of pests. Implement preventative measures such as screens on windows and doors, and use professional pest control services if necessary.

5. **Allergen Management**

If you offer products that contain common allergens such as nuts, dairy, or gluten, it is essential to manage the risk of cross-contamination. Clearly label products that contain allergens and implement strict procedures for cleaning and separating equipment used for allergen-free baking.

Conclusion

Setting up your home kitchen efficiently and safely is crucial for the success of your baking business. By organizing your workspace, investing in essential equipment, and adhering to health and safety standards, you can create an environment that supports high-quality production and ensures customer satisfaction. With your kitchen ready, you are well-prepared to start baking and building your business.

Chapter 4: Legal Requirements and Permits

Starting a home baking business involves more than just creating delicious treats; it also requires complying with various legal requirements and obtaining the necessary permits. Ensuring that your business operates legally is crucial to avoid fines, shutdowns, and potential legal issues. In this chapter, we will guide you through the essential legal steps to take before launching your home baking business.

Understanding Local Regulations

The first step in navigating the legal landscape of your home baking business is to understand the regulations in your area. These regulations vary widely depending on your location, so it is essential to research the specific requirements that apply to your business.

1. Cottage Food Laws

Many regions have cottage food laws that allow individuals to prepare and sell certain low-risk foods from their home kitchens. These laws are designed to support small-scale food entrepreneurs while ensuring public safety. Cottage food laws typically specify which types of foods can be produced at home, such as baked goods, jams, and candies. They also outline the labeling requirements, sales limits, and restrictions on where products can be sold.

To find out if your area has cottage food laws, contact your local health department or food safety authority. They can provide you with detailed information on the types of products allowed, as well as any additional requirements you need to meet.

2. Business Licensing

In addition to cottage food laws, you will need to obtain a business license to operate legally. A business license is a government-issued permit that allows you to conduct business within a specific jurisdiction. The process for obtaining a business license varies depending on your location, but generally involves:

- Completing an application form with details about your business.
- Paying a fee, which can vary based on your business type and location.
- Complying with local zoning regulations, which determine where businesses can operate.

Contact your local city or county clerk's office to find out how to apply for a business license in your area.

3. Health Department Permits

Even if your region has cottage food laws, you may still need to obtain permits from your local health department. These permits ensure that your home kitchen meets health and safety standards for food production. The requirements for health department permits can include:

- Passing a kitchen inspection to ensure cleanliness and proper food handling practices.
- Completing a food safety training course and obtaining a food handler's permit.
- Complying with specific guidelines for ingredient storage, equipment use, and waste disposal.

Your local health department can provide you with information on the specific requirements and procedures for obtaining the necessary permits.

4. Sales Tax Permits

If you plan to sell your baked goods, you may be required to collect and remit sales tax. A sales tax permit, also known as a seller's permit or sales tax license, allows you to charge sales tax on your products and submit it to the government. The process for obtaining a sales tax permit typically involves:

- Registering with your state's tax authority.
- Providing information about your business, including your estimated sales.
- Reporting and remitting sales tax on a regular basis, such as monthly or quarterly.

Consult your state's tax authority for details on how to register for a sales tax permit and understand your tax obligations.

5. Business Insurance

While not always legally required, obtaining business insurance is a wise decision to protect your home baking business from potential risks. Business insurance can cover various aspects of your operation, including:

- General liability insurance to protect against claims of bodily injury or property damage.
- Product liability insurance to cover issues related to your baked goods, such as foodborne illness or allergic reactions.

- Property insurance to protect your equipment and supplies in case of damage or theft.

Speak with an insurance agent who specializes in small businesses to find the right coverage for your needs.

Labeling and Packaging Requirements

Proper labeling and packaging are essential for compliance with legal regulations and for building customer trust. Here are some key labeling requirements to keep in mind:

1. Ingredient List

Include a complete list of ingredients on your product labels. This helps customers with allergies or dietary restrictions make informed choices. List ingredients in descending order of weight, from the most to the least.

2. Allergen Information

Clearly identify any common allergens in your products, such as nuts, dairy, eggs, soy, wheat, and gluten. Use bold or capitalized text to highlight allergen information and consider including a separate allergen statement on your labels.

3. Net Weight or Quantity

Include the net weight or quantity of your product on the label. This information helps customers understand how much they are purchasing and ensures compliance with packaging regulations.

4. Business Information

Provide your business name, address, and contact information on your labels. This not only complies with legal requirements but also helps customers reach you with questions or feedback.

5. Cottage Food Statement

If you are operating under cottage food laws, you may be required to include a specific statement on your labels, such as "Made in a home kitchen" or "This product was produced in a home kitchen not subject to inspection." Check your local regulations for the exact wording required.

Maintaining Compliance

Staying compliant with legal requirements is an ongoing process. Here are some tips to ensure your business remains in good standing:

1. Keep Detailed Records

Maintain accurate records of your business operations, including ingredient purchases, sales transactions, and financial statements. Detailed records can help you manage your business effectively and provide documentation in case of inspections or audits.

2. Stay Informed

Laws and regulations can change over time, so it is important to stay informed about any updates that may affect your business. Subscribe to newsletters or join local business associations to receive the latest information on legal requirements and industry trends.

3. Renew Permits and Licenses

Ensure that all your permits and licenses are up to date. Mark renewal dates on your calendar and complete any necessary paperwork or inspections well in advance to avoid lapses in coverage.

4. Seek Professional Advice

If you have questions or concerns about legal compliance, consider seeking advice from professionals such as lawyers, accountants, or business consultants. They can provide guidance tailored to your specific situation and help you navigate complex legal requirements.

Conclusion

Complying with legal requirements and obtaining the necessary permits are crucial steps in starting your home baking business. By understanding and adhering to local regulations, you can operate legally and build a solid foundation for your business. With the legal aspects in order, you are well-prepared to focus on creating delicious baked goods and growing your business.

In the next chapter, we will discuss how to create a comprehensive business plan that outlines your goals, target market, and strategies for success. Let's continue on this journey to turn your passion into a successful enterprise!

Chapter 5: Creating a Business Plan

A well-crafted business plan is essential for the success of your home baking business. It serves as a roadmap, guiding you through the various stages of your business development and helping you stay focused on your goals. In this chapter, we will explore the key components of a business plan and how to create one tailored to your home baking business.

The Importance of a Business Plan

A business plan is more than just a document; it is a strategic tool that helps you clarify your vision, set realistic goals, and outline the steps needed to achieve them. It also serves as a valuable resource when seeking funding or partnerships, as it demonstrates your commitment and preparedness to potential investors and collaborators.

Components of a Business Plan

1. **Executive Summary**

The executive summary is a concise overview of your business plan. It should provide a snapshot of your business, including your mission statement, key objectives, and a brief description of your products and services. While the executive summary appears at the beginning of the business plan, it is often written last, after the other sections are completed.

2. **Business Description**

In this section, provide a detailed description of your home baking business. Include information about your business structure (sole proprietorship, partnership, LLC), your location, and the history of your business. Describe your niche and unique selling proposition (USP) that sets you apart from competitors.

3. **Market Analysis**

Conduct a thorough market analysis to understand the industry landscape and identify your target market. Include information on market size, trends, and growth potential. Analyze your competitors, highlighting their strengths and weaknesses, and explain how you plan to position your business to gain a competitive advantage.

4. **Organization and Management**

Outline the organizational structure of your business, including key roles and responsibilities. If you have a team, provide information about their qualifications and experience. If you are a solo entrepreneur, explain how you plan to manage different aspects of the business, such as production, marketing, and customer service.

5. **Products and Services**

Provide a detailed description of the products and services you offer. Highlight your signature items and explain how they meet the needs of your target market. Include information on your production process, ingredient sourcing, and any unique features or benefits of your products.

6. **Marketing and Sales Strategy**

Develop a comprehensive marketing and sales strategy to promote your business and attract customers. Include details on your branding, pricing, and promotional tactics. Explain how you plan to reach your target audience through online and offline channels, such as social media, your website, local events, and partnerships.

7. **Operational Plan**

Describe the day-to-day operations of your business. Include information on your production schedule, inventory management, and order fulfillment process. Outline any equipment and supplies you need, and explain how you plan to maintain quality and consistency in your products.

8. **Financial Plan**

The financial plan is a crucial component of your business plan, outlining your revenue model, expenses, and financial projections. Include a startup budget, detailing the initial costs of setting up your business, such as equipment, ingredients, permits, and marketing. Provide projected income statements, cash flow statements, and balance sheets for the first few years of operation.

9. **Funding Request**

If you are seeking funding, include a section on your funding request. Specify the amount of funding you need, how you plan to use it, and the terms you are offering to investors or lenders. Explain how the funding will help you achieve your business goals and provide a return on investment.

Tips for Writing a Business Plan

1. **Be Realistic**

Set realistic goals and projections in your business plan. While it is important to be ambitious, avoid overly optimistic assumptions that may not be achievable. Use conservative estimates and consider potential challenges and risks.

2. **Be Specific**

Provide specific details and examples to support your claims and projections. Use data and research to back up your market analysis and financial forecasts. The more specific and well-researched your plan, the more credible it will be to potential investors and partners.

3. **Be Clear and Concise**

Write your business plan in clear, concise language that is easy to understand. Avoid jargon and technical terms that may confuse readers. Use headings and subheadings to organize the content and make it easy to navigate.

4. **Review and Revise**

A business plan is a living document that should be reviewed and revised regularly. As your business evolves, update your plan to reflect changes in your goals, strategies, and market conditions. Regularly reviewing your plan will help you stay on track and make informed decisions.

Conclusion

Creating a comprehensive business plan is a critical step in building a successful home baking business. By outlining your vision, goals, and strategies, you can navigate the challenges of entrepreneurship with confidence and clarity. With a solid business plan in place, you are well-prepared to launch and grow your home baking business.

In the next chapter, we will delve into the financial aspects of running a home baking business, including pricing your products, managing costs, and understanding profitability. Let's continue on this journey to turn your passion into a successful enterprise!

Chapter 6: Pricing Your Products and Understanding Profitability

Pricing your products correctly is crucial for the success of your home baking business. Setting the right price helps you cover costs, achieve profitability, and provide value to your customers. In this chapter, we will explore strategies for pricing your baked goods, managing costs, and understanding profitability.

Understanding Your Costs

Before you can set your prices, it is essential to understand the costs involved in producing your baked goods. These costs can be categorized into two main types: fixed costs and variable costs.

1. **Fixed Costs**

Fixed costs are expenses that remain constant regardless of the number of goods you produce. These include:

- **Rent or Mortgage:** If you are using a dedicated space for your baking business, such as a commercial kitchen or a separate area in your home, the rent or mortgage payments are considered fixed costs.
- **Utilities:** Electricity, water, and gas bills are fixed costs that support your baking operations.
- **Insurance:** Business insurance premiums are fixed costs that protect your business from potential risks.
- **Licenses and Permits:** Fees for obtaining and renewing business licenses and permits are fixed costs.
- **Marketing Expenses:** Costs for ongoing marketing efforts, such as website hosting, social media advertising, and promotional materials, are fixed expenses.

2. Variable Costs

Variable costs fluctuate based on the volume of goods you produce. These include:

- **Ingredients:** The cost of ingredients such as flour, sugar, butter, eggs, and flavorings varies with the quantity of products you make.
- **Packaging:** Expenses for packaging materials like boxes, bags, labels, and ribbons depend on the number of items you sell.
- **Labor:** If you hire additional help for baking, decorating, or delivering your products, labor costs are variable.
- **Shipping and Delivery:** Costs for shipping supplies and delivery services vary based on the number of orders and their destinations.

Calculating Your Cost Per Unit

To set profitable prices, you need to calculate your cost per unit for each product. Here's how to do it:

1. List All Ingredients and Quantities

Create a detailed list of all ingredients used in a specific recipe, including their quantities. For example, if you are baking a batch of cookies, list the amount of flour, sugar, butter, eggs, and any other ingredients needed.

2. Determine the Cost of Each Ingredient

Find out the cost of each ingredient by checking your purchase receipts or supplier invoices. Divide the total cost by the quantity purchased to get the cost per unit of each ingredient. For example, if a 5-pound bag of flour costs $3, and you use 2 cups of flour for the recipe, calculate the cost of 2 cups.

3. **Calculate the Total Ingredient Cost**

Add up the costs of all the ingredients used in the recipe to get the total ingredient cost. This gives you the variable cost for producing one batch of the product.

4. **Include Packaging Costs**

Add the cost of packaging materials for one unit of the product. For example, if you use a box, label, and ribbon for packaging, calculate the total cost of these materials.

5. **Account for Overhead Costs**

Divide your fixed costs by the number of units you expect to produce over a specific period (e.g., monthly or yearly) to get the overhead cost per unit. Add this to the variable cost to get the total cost per unit.

6. **Add Labor Costs**

If you pay yourself or any employees for the time spent baking and decorating, calculate the labor cost per unit and add it to the total cost.

Setting Your Prices

Once you have calculated your cost per unit, you can set your prices. Consider the following factors when determining your prices:

1. **Market Research**

Conduct market research to understand the pricing landscape for similar products in your area. Look at the prices charged by competitors and consider the quality and uniqueness of their offerings. Use this information to gauge a reasonable price range for your products.

2. **Value Proposition**

Consider the value your products offer to customers. Factors such as taste, quality, presentation, and uniqueness can justify higher prices. Communicate the value of your products through your branding and marketing efforts.

3. **Profit Margin**

Decide on your desired profit margin, which is the percentage of profit you want to make on each product. A typical profit margin for baked goods ranges from 20% to 50%. Add the desired profit margin to your cost per unit to determine the selling price.

4. **Customer Perception**

Consider how your prices will be perceived by customers. Prices that are too high may deter customers, while prices that are too low may undermine the perceived quality of your products. Strive for a balance that reflects the value of your offerings and attracts your target market.

Pricing Strategies

Here are some common pricing strategies you can use for your home baking business:

1. **Cost-Plus Pricing**

This straightforward approach involves adding a markup to your cost per unit to determine the selling price. For example, if your cost per unit is $2 and you want a 50% profit margin, your selling price would be $3.

2. **Competitive Pricing**

Set your prices based on the prices charged by competitors. This strategy works well if you operate in a competitive market with similar products. Ensure that your prices are competitive while still covering your costs and achieving profitability.

3. **Value-Based Pricing**

Price your products based on the perceived value to customers. This approach is suitable if your products offer unique qualities or benefits that justify higher prices. Communicate the value through your branding and marketing efforts.

4. **Bundle Pricing**

Offer bundled deals where customers can purchase multiple products at a discounted price. For example, sell a dozen cookies at a lower price than buying individual cookies. Bundle pricing can encourage higher sales volumes and attract customers looking for value.

5. **Seasonal Pricing**

Adjust your prices based on seasonal demand. For example, you can charge higher prices for holiday-themed baked goods or offer discounts during slower periods. Seasonal pricing helps maximize profits during peak times and boost sales during off-peak periods.

Monitoring and Adjusting Prices

Once you have set your prices, it is important to monitor their effectiveness and make adjustments as needed. Here are some tips for managing your pricing strategy:

1. **Track Sales and Profitability**

Regularly review your sales data and financial statements to assess the performance of your pricing strategy. Track the profitability of each product and identify any areas where adjustments may be needed.

2. **Gather Customer Feedback**

Pay attention to customer feedback regarding your prices. If customers consistently comment on high prices or express willingness to pay more for certain products, use this feedback to refine your pricing strategy.

3. **Analyze Market Trends**

Stay informed about market trends and competitor pricing. Adjust your prices to remain competitive and capitalize on emerging opportunities.

4. **Test Price Changes**

Experiment with small price changes to gauge their impact on sales and profitability. Monitor the results and use the insights to make informed pricing decisions.

Conclusion

Pricing your products effectively is essential for the profitability and success of your home baking business. By understanding your costs, conducting market research, and choosing the right pricing strategy, you can set prices that attract customers and achieve your financial goals. With a well-thought-out pricing strategy, you are well-prepared to grow your business and enjoy the rewards of your hard work.

In the next chapter, we will explore marketing strategies to promote your home baking business and attract a loyal customer base. Let's continue on this journey to turn your passion into a successful enterprise!

Chapter 7: Marketing Strategies to Promote Your Home Baking Business

Effective marketing is essential for building awareness, attracting customers, and growing your home baking business. In this chapter, we will explore various marketing strategies to promote your business and create a loyal customer base.

Building Your Brand

Your brand is the identity of your business, encompassing your logo, colors, messaging, and overall image. A strong brand helps you stand out from competitors and create a memorable impression on customers. Here's how to build a compelling brand for your home baking business:

1. **Define Your Brand Identity**

Start by defining your brand identity. Consider what makes your business unique and what values you want to convey. Think about your target audience and what appeals to them. Your brand identity should reflect the personality and style of your business.

2. **Create a Logo and Visual Identity**

Design a professional logo that represents your brand. Choose colors, fonts, and design elements that align with your brand identity. Use your logo consistently across all marketing materials, including your website, social media profiles, packaging, and promotional items.

3. **Craft Your Brand Message**

Develop a clear and compelling brand message that communicates the essence of your business. Your message should highlight your unique selling points, such as the quality of your ingredients, the care you put into your products, or the creativity of your designs. Use this message consistently in your marketing efforts.

Establishing an Online Presence

In today's digital age, having an online presence is crucial for reaching potential customers and building your brand. Here are some key strategies for establishing and enhancing your online presence:

1. **Create a Professional Website**

A professional website serves as the online hub for your business. It should include:

- **Home Page:** An engaging introduction to your business, highlighting your products and unique selling points.
- **About Page:** A page that tells your story and shares your background, mission, and values.
- **Product Pages:** Detailed descriptions and high-quality images of your products, along with pricing and ordering information.

- **Contact Page:** Information on how customers can reach you, including an email address, phone number, and social media links.
- **Blog:** A blog where you can share recipes, baking tips, and behind-the-scenes stories, helping you connect with your audience and improve your website's search engine ranking.

2. **Utilize Social Media**

Social media platforms are powerful tools for promoting your business and engaging with customers. Choose platforms that align with your target audience and focus on creating engaging content. Here are some tips for using social media effectively:

- **Post Regularly:** Share updates, product photos, behind-the-scenes content, and customer testimonials regularly to keep your audience engaged.
- **Use Hashtags:** Use relevant hashtags to increase the visibility of your posts and attract new followers.
- **Engage with Followers:** Respond to comments, messages, and reviews promptly. Engaging with your audience builds relationships and fosters loyalty.
- **Run Promotions:** Use social media to announce special offers, giveaways, and contests to encourage participation and boost sales.

3. **Leverage Email Marketing**

Email marketing is an effective way to communicate directly with your customers. Build an email list by offering incentives such as discounts or free recipes in exchange for signing up. Send regular newsletters with updates, promotions, and valuable content. Personalize your emails to make your customers feel valued and appreciated.

Local Marketing Strategies

In addition to online marketing, local marketing strategies can help you reach customers in your community. Here are some ideas for promoting your home baking business locally:

1. **Participate in Local Events**

Join local events such as farmers' markets, craft fairs, and food festivals to showcase your products and connect with potential customers. These events provide opportunities for face-to-face interactions and allow customers to sample your baked goods.

2. **Partner with Local Businesses**

Collaborate with local businesses, such as coffee shops, restaurants, and boutiques, to feature your products. This can help you reach new customers and build partnerships within your community.

3. **Distribute Flyers and Business Cards**

Create eye-catching flyers and business cards to distribute in your local area. Place them in strategic locations such as community centers, libraries, and bulletin boards. Include your contact information and a compelling call to action.

4. **Offer Local Delivery**

Providing local delivery services can make it convenient for customers to order from you. Promote your delivery options on your website, social media, and local listings.

Building Customer Relationships

Building strong relationships with your customers is key to creating a loyal customer base. Here are some strategies for fostering customer loyalty:

1. **Provide Excellent Customer Service**

Deliver exceptional customer service at every touchpoint. Be responsive, friendly, and accommodating to customer inquiries and requests. Address any issues promptly and professionally.

2. **Offer Loyalty Programs**

Implement a loyalty program to reward repeat customers. Offer incentives such as discounts, free products, or exclusive access to new items. Loyalty programs encourage repeat business and make customers feel appreciated.

3. **Collect and Showcase Testimonials**

Ask satisfied customers for testimonials and reviews. Showcase these positive comments on your website, social media, and marketing materials. Testimonials build credibility and trust with potential customers.

4. **Engage with Your Community**

Engage with your local community by participating in charity events, sponsoring local causes, and supporting community initiatives. Being involved in your community enhances your brand's reputation and fosters goodwill.

Analyzing and Adjusting Your Marketing Strategy

Regularly analyze the effectiveness of your marketing efforts to ensure they are driving results. Use analytics tools to track website traffic, social media engagement, and email open rates. Collect feedback from customers to understand what is working and what can be improved. Use this data to refine your marketing strategy and achieve better results.

Conclusion

Effective marketing is essential for the growth and success of your home baking business. By building a strong brand, establishing an online presence, utilizing local marketing strategies, and fostering customer relationships, you can attract and retain loyal customers. With a well-executed marketing plan, you are well-prepared to take your business to new heights.

In the next chapter, we will explore the operational aspects of running your home baking business, including production processes, inventory management, and quality control. Let's continue on this journey to turn your passion into a successful enterprise!

Chapter 8 : Operational Aspects of Running Your Home Baking Business

Efficient operations are critical to the success of your home baking business. From production processes to inventory management and quality control, effective operations ensure that your products meet high standards and that your business runs smoothly. In this chapter, we will explore the key operational aspects of managing your home baking business.

Setting Up Your Production Space

Creating an efficient and organized production space is essential for productivity and maintaining hygiene standards. Here are some steps to set up your baking area:

1. **Designate a Dedicated Baking Area**

Choose a specific area in your home for baking. Ensure that it is separate from your personal living space to comply with health regulations and maintain a professional environment. A dedicated baking area helps you stay organized and focused on your work.

2. **Invest in Quality Equipment**

Purchase high-quality baking equipment that suits your needs. Essential items include an oven, mixer, baking sheets, pans, measuring tools, and cooling racks. Invest in durable and reliable equipment to ensure consistent results and efficiency in your baking process.

3. **Organize Your Workspace**

Keep your workspace tidy and organized. Use shelves, cabinets, and storage containers to store ingredients, tools, and packaging materials. Label everything clearly to save time and reduce the risk of errors.

4. **Ensure Proper Ventilation**

Good ventilation is crucial for maintaining a comfortable and safe baking environment. Ensure that your kitchen has proper airflow to prevent the buildup of heat and odors. Install an exhaust fan or open windows to improve ventilation.

Establishing Efficient Production Processes

Streamlined production processes help you produce high-quality baked goods efficiently. Here are some tips for optimizing your production workflow:

1. **Plan Your Production Schedule**

Create a production schedule that outlines your baking tasks for the week or month. Plan your baking sessions based on order deadlines, peak demand times, and the shelf life of your products. A well-structured schedule helps you manage your time effectively and meet customer expectations.

2. **Batch Production**

Consider baking in batches to save time and reduce waste. Group similar products together and bake them in larger quantities. Batch production is especially useful for items with longer shelf lives, such as cookies and cakes.

3. **Prep Ingredients in Advance**

Prepare your ingredients in advance to streamline your baking process. Measure and portion out ingredients ahead of time, and store them in labeled containers. This reduces prep time and minimizes the risk of errors during baking.

4. **Use Standardized Recipes**

Standardize your recipes to ensure consistency in taste and quality. Follow precise measurements and instructions for each recipe. Keep a record of your standardized recipes for reference and training purposes.

5. **Implement Quality Control Checks**

Establish quality control checks at various stages of your production process. Inspect ingredients for freshness and quality before use. Monitor the baking process to ensure products are cooked to perfection. Conduct a final inspection of finished products to check for appearance, taste, and packaging quality.

Inventory Management

Effective inventory management ensures that you have the necessary ingredients and supplies on hand without overstocking. Here are some strategies for managing your inventory:

1. **Track Your Inventory**

Maintain an inventory tracking system to monitor your stock levels. Use spreadsheets or inventory management software to record the quantities of ingredients, packaging materials, and finished products. Update your inventory records regularly to keep track of stock levels and usage.

2. **Implement First-In, First-Out (FIFO)**

Follow the FIFO method to manage your inventory. Use older stock before newer stock to prevent spoilage and waste. Arrange your inventory storage to facilitate the FIFO method, with older items at the front and newer items at the back.

3. **Set Reorder Points**

Establish reorder points for each ingredient and supply. Determine the minimum stock level required to maintain production and set reorder points accordingly. When inventory reaches the reorder point, place orders with your suppliers to replenish stock.

4. **Monitor Shelf Life**

Keep track of the shelf life of your ingredients and finished products. Use labels or stickers to indicate expiration dates. Regularly check your inventory for items nearing their expiration dates and prioritize their use.

5. **Manage Supplier Relationships**

Build strong relationships with your suppliers to ensure timely and reliable deliveries. Communicate your inventory needs and order quantities clearly. Negotiate favorable terms and prices to optimize your purchasing process.

Quality Control and Consistency

Maintaining high-quality standards is essential for building customer trust and loyalty. Here are some tips for ensuring quality and consistency in your baked goods:

1. **Source High-Quality Ingredients**

Use high-quality ingredients to produce superior products. Choose reputable suppliers and verify the quality of ingredients before use. Avoid cutting corners on ingredient quality, as it directly impacts the taste and appearance of your baked goods.

2. **Maintain Cleanliness and Hygiene**

Adhere to strict cleanliness and hygiene standards in your baking area. Regularly clean and sanitize your equipment, surfaces, and utensils. Follow food safety guidelines to prevent contamination and ensure the safety of your products.

3. **Train Your Team**

If you have a team, provide training to ensure that everyone follows standardized procedures and quality control measures. Conduct regular training sessions to keep your team updated on best practices and new techniques.

4. **Conduct Taste Tests**

Regularly conduct taste tests to evaluate the flavor, texture, and appearance of your products. Gather feedback from customers, friends, and family to identify areas for improvement. Use this feedback to refine your recipes and production processes.

5. **Document Quality Control Procedures**

Create a quality control manual that outlines your procedures for ensuring product quality. Include checklists, guidelines, and standard operating procedures (SOPs) for each stage of production. Use this manual as a reference for training and maintaining consistency.

Managing Orders and Fulfillment

Efficient order management and fulfillment are crucial for customer satisfaction. Here are some tips for managing orders and ensuring timely delivery:

1. **Implement an Order Management System**

Use an order management system to track and process customer orders. This system should allow you to record order details, track order status, and manage inventory levels. Choose a system that integrates with your website and payment platforms for seamless order processing.

2. **Set Clear Lead Times**

Establish clear lead times for order processing and delivery. Communicate these lead times to customers on your website and during the ordering process. Ensure that you can meet these lead times consistently to maintain customer satisfaction.

3. **Prepare for Peak Times**

Anticipate peak times, such as holidays and special events, and plan your production schedule accordingly. Increase your inventory of popular items and prepare for a higher volume of orders. Consider hiring additional help during busy periods to manage the increased workload.

4. **Ensure Accurate Order Fulfillment**

Double-check each order before packaging and shipping to ensure accuracy. Verify that the correct items, quantities, and packaging are used. Implement a checklist system to minimize errors and ensure that all orders are fulfilled correctly.

5. **Offer Multiple Delivery Options**

Provide customers with multiple delivery options, such as standard shipping, expedited shipping, and local delivery. Clearly communicate the delivery times and costs for each option. Use reliable shipping carriers to ensure timely and safe delivery of your products.

Conclusion

Efficient operations are the backbone of a successful home baking business. By setting up a well-organized production space, establishing efficient production processes, managing inventory effectively, maintaining high-quality standards, and ensuring accurate order fulfillment, you can build a reputation for excellence and reliability. With a focus on operational efficiency, you are well-equipped to meet customer expectations and grow your business.

In the next chapter, we will explore the legal and regulatory aspects of running a home baking business, including permits, licenses, and compliance with health and safety regulations. Let's continue on this journey to turn your passion into a successful enterprise!

Chapter 9: Navigating Legal and Regulatory Requirements

Understanding and complying with legal and regulatory requirements is essential for running a legitimate and successful home baking business. In this chapter, we will explore the key legal aspects you need to consider, including permits, licenses, health and safety regulations, and intellectual property protection.

Understanding Local Regulations

Before you start your home baking business, it is crucial to familiarize yourself with local regulations that govern home-based food businesses. Regulations vary by location, so you need to research the specific requirements in your area. Here are some common regulatory aspects to consider:

1. **Zoning Laws**

Zoning laws determine whether you can legally operate a business from your home. Check with your local zoning office or city planning department to understand the zoning regulations in your area. Some residential areas may have restrictions on commercial activities, while others may allow home-based businesses with certain conditions.

2. **Cottage Food Laws**

Cottage food laws are regulations that govern the production and sale of homemade food products. These laws vary by state and locality, so you need to understand the specific requirements in your area. Cottage food laws typically cover:

- **Types of Products Allowed:** Some cottage food laws restrict the types of products you can sell, such as baked goods, jams, and candies.
- **Sales Limits:** There may be limits on the amount of revenue you can generate or the volume of products you can sell.
- **Labeling Requirements:** Cottage food laws often require specific labeling for homemade products, including ingredient lists, allergen information, and disclaimers.

3. **Health and Safety Regulations**

Health and safety regulations ensure that your food products are safe for consumption. These regulations cover aspects such as kitchen cleanliness, food handling practices, and sanitation. Key health and safety considerations include:

- **Kitchen Inspections:** Some local health departments require regular inspections of your home kitchen to ensure it meets hygiene standards.
- **Food Handling Certification:** You may need to obtain a food handler's certificate or complete a food safety course to demonstrate your knowledge of safe food handling practices.

- **Sanitation Practices:** Implement strict sanitation practices in your kitchen, including regular cleaning, proper food storage, and preventing cross-contamination.

Obtaining Permits and Licenses

To operate your home baking business legally, you may need to obtain various permits and licenses. The specific requirements depend on your location and the nature of your business. Common permits and licenses include:

1. **Business License**

A business license is a general permit that allows you to operate a business within your locality. Contact your local government office to apply for a business license. You may need to provide information about your business, such as its name, address, and type of operation.

2. **Home Occupation Permit**

A home occupation permit allows you to run a business from your home. This permit ensures that your business activities comply with local zoning laws. Check with your city or county zoning office to apply for a home occupation permit.

3. **Health Department Permit**

If your local health department regulates home-based food businesses, you may need to obtain a health department permit. This permit often requires passing a kitchen inspection and demonstrating compliance with health and safety regulations.

4. **Sales Tax Permit**

If you plan to sell your baked goods, you may need to collect sales tax. Apply for a sales tax permit from your state's revenue department to legally collect and remit sales tax on your products.

5. **Food Establishment License**

In some areas, you may need a food establishment license to operate a home-based food business. This license is typically required for businesses that prepare and sell food products. Contact your local health department for specific requirements and application procedures.

Complying with Labeling Requirements

Proper labeling of your baked goods is essential for compliance with regulations and for providing important information to your customers. Here are key labeling requirements to consider:

1. **Ingredient List**

Include a complete list of ingredients on your product labels. List ingredients in descending order by weight, and use common names for each ingredient. This helps customers understand what is in your products and identify any potential allergens.

2. **Allergen Information**

Clearly indicate the presence of common allergens such as nuts, dairy, eggs, soy, and wheat. Use bold font or a separate allergen statement to highlight these ingredients. Accurate allergen labeling is crucial for the safety of customers with food allergies.

3. **Net Weight**

Include the net weight or volume of your products on the label. Use standard units of measurement, such as ounces or grams, to indicate the quantity of the product. This information helps customers make informed purchasing decisions.

4. **Business Information**

Include your business name, address, and contact information on the label. This provides customers with a way to reach you if they have questions or concerns about your products. It also adds a professional touch to your packaging.

5. **Cottage Food Disclaimer**

If required by local cottage food laws, include a disclaimer on your labels indicating that your products were made in a home kitchen. This disclaimer informs customers that your products are homemade and not subject to the same regulations as commercial food establishments.

Intellectual Property Protection

Protecting your intellectual property helps safeguard your brand and products. Here are some steps to protect your intellectual property:

1. **Trademark Your Brand**

Consider trademarking your business name, logo, and any unique product names. A trademark provides legal protection against unauthorized use of your brand identity. Consult with an intellectual property attorney to guide you through the trademark registration process.

2. **Copyright Your Recipes**

While it is challenging to copyright a recipe itself, you can copyright the written expression of your recipes, such as the detailed instructions and creative presentation. This provides some level of protection for your original creations.

3. **Maintain Trade Secrets**

Keep your unique recipes and techniques confidential to protect them as trade secrets. Limit access to this information to trusted individuals and avoid sharing it publicly. Use non-disclosure agreements (NDAs) if you need to share proprietary information with others.

Insurance Coverage

Insurance provides financial protection against potential risks and liabilities. Consider the following types of insurance for your home baking business:

1. **General Liability Insurance**

General liability insurance covers claims related to third-party injuries, property damage, and advertising injuries. This insurance protects you in case a customer becomes ill after consuming your products or if someone is injured on your property.

2. **Product Liability Insurance**

Product liability insurance specifically covers claims related to your products. It provides protection if a customer experiences harm or injury due to consuming your baked goods. This insurance is essential for any business that sells food products.

3. **Business Property Insurance**

Business property insurance covers damage to your business property, such as equipment, supplies, and inventory. It provides financial protection in case of events such as fire, theft, or natural disasters.

4. **Commercial Auto Insurance**

If you use a vehicle for business purposes, such as delivering products, consider obtaining commercial auto insurance. This insurance covers accidents and damages involving your business vehicle.

Conclusion

Navigating legal and regulatory requirements is a critical aspect of running a successful home baking business. By understanding and complying with local regulations, obtaining necessary permits and licenses, adhering to labeling requirements, protecting your intellectual property, and securing appropriate insurance coverage, you can operate your business legally and protect yourself from potential risks.

In the next chapter, we will explore financial management and bookkeeping practices for your home baking business. Effective financial management is essential for maintaining profitability and ensuring the long-term success of your business. Let's continue on this journey to turn your passion into a successful enterprise!

Chapter 10: Financial Management and Bookkeeping Practices

Effective financial management is crucial for the success and sustainability of your home baking business. In this chapter, we will explore essential financial principles, bookkeeping practices, budgeting techniques, pricing strategies, and tips for managing cash flow.

Understanding Financial Principles

To effectively manage your finances, it's important to understand key financial principles that apply to your home baking business:

1. **Revenue and Expenses**

Revenue refers to the income generated from selling your baked goods, while expenses are the costs incurred in running your business. Track both your revenue and expenses to assess your business's financial performance accurately.

2. **Profitability**

Profitability measures your business's ability to generate income relative to its expenses. Calculate your profitability by subtracting total expenses from total revenue. Aim to achieve consistent profitability to sustain and grow your business.

3. **Cash Flow**

Cash flow refers to the movement of money in and out of your business. It's essential to manage cash flow effectively to ensure you have enough liquidity to cover expenses and invest in business growth. Monitor your cash flow regularly to avoid cash shortages.

4. **Financial Statements**

Financial statements, such as income statements, balance sheets, and cash flow statements, provide a snapshot of your business's financial health. These statements summarize revenue, expenses, assets, liabilities, and cash flow over a specific period. Use financial statements to analyze trends, make informed decisions, and plan for the future.

Implementing Effective Bookkeeping Practices

Accurate bookkeeping is essential for maintaining financial records and tracking your business's financial transactions. Follow these practices to establish effective bookkeeping:

1. **Use Accounting Software**

Invest in accounting software to streamline bookkeeping tasks and maintain organized financial records. Accounting software automates processes such as invoicing, expense tracking, and financial reporting. Choose software that meets your business's needs and integrates with other tools.

2. **Track Income and Expenses**

Record all income and expenses related to your home baking business accurately. Categorize transactions to distinguish between different types of income (e.g., sales revenue) and expenses (e.g., ingredients, packaging, utilities). This helps you monitor cash flow and assess financial performance.

3. **Reconcile Bank Accounts Regularly**

Reconcile your business bank accounts regularly to ensure that your accounting records match your bank statements. Compare transactions, identify discrepancies, and address any errors promptly. Reconciliation helps maintain accuracy in your financial records.

4. **Maintain Separate Accounts**

Separate your personal and business finances by maintaining separate bank accounts and credit cards. This simplifies bookkeeping, facilitates tax preparation, and ensures transparency in your business's financial activities.

5. **Track Inventory**

If you maintain inventory of ingredients, packaging materials, or finished products, track inventory levels accurately. Use inventory management tools to monitor stock levels, track usage, and reorder supplies as needed. Proper inventory management prevents stockouts and reduces waste.

Budgeting Techniques

Budgeting allows you to plan and allocate financial resources effectively. Develop a budget to guide your spending and achieve your business goals:

1. **Revenue Projections**

Estimate your expected revenue based on sales forecasts, pricing strategies, and market demand. Consider seasonal fluctuations and promotional activities that may impact revenue.

2. **Expense Budget**

Identify and budget for recurring expenses such as ingredients, packaging, utilities, equipment maintenance, and marketing. Allocate funds for one-time expenses or investments in business growth.

3. **Profit Margin Analysis**

Calculate your profit margins to assess the profitability of your products. Determine the cost of goods sold (COGS) for each product and subtract it from the selling price to calculate gross profit margin. Aim to maintain healthy profit margins to cover expenses and generate profit.

4. **Cash Flow Forecast**

Create a cash flow forecast to project inflows and outflows of cash over a specific period, such as monthly or quarterly. Anticipate timing of income from sales and expenses such as supplier payments, rent, and taxes. Use cash flow forecasts to identify potential cash shortages or surpluses and plan accordingly.

Pricing Strategies

Setting appropriate prices for your baked goods is crucial for profitability and competitiveness. Consider these pricing strategies:

1. **Cost-Based Pricing**

Calculate the cost of ingredients, packaging, labor, and overhead costs to determine the minimum price for your products. Add a markup or profit margin to cover expenses and generate profit. Ensure that your prices reflect the value perceived by customers.

2. **Competitive Pricing**

Research competitors' pricing for similar products in your market. Set prices that are competitive while considering factors such as product quality, uniqueness, and customer preferences. Differentiate your products based on value-added features or premium ingredients.

3. **Value-Based Pricing**

Set prices based on the perceived value of your products to customers. Consider factors such as product quality, taste, brand reputation, and customer service. Align prices with the value customers place on your baked goods to justify higher prices for premium offerings.

4. **Promotional Pricing**

Offer promotional pricing strategies such as discounts, bundling deals, or seasonal promotions to attract customers and stimulate sales. Monitor the impact of promotional pricing on profitability and adjust strategies based on customer response.

Managing Cash Flow

Maintaining healthy cash flow is essential for sustaining operations and managing financial obligations. Use these tips to manage cash flow effectively:

1. **Monitor Receivables and Payables**

Track accounts receivable (money owed to your business) and accounts payable (money your business owes to suppliers and vendors). Follow up on overdue payments from customers and negotiate favorable payment terms with suppliers to improve cash flow.

2. **Control Expenses**

Manage expenses by prioritizing necessary expenditures and reducing discretionary spending. Negotiate discounts with suppliers, compare prices for major purchases, and review recurring expenses regularly to identify cost-saving opportunities.

3. **Forecast and Plan for Expenses**

Anticipate upcoming expenses such as equipment maintenance, inventory replenishment, and seasonal fluctuations in demand. Incorporate these expenses into your budget and cash flow forecast to ensure sufficient funds are available when needed.

4. **Build a Cash Reserve**

Maintain a cash reserve or emergency fund to cover unexpected expenses or temporary cash shortages. Set aside a portion of revenue regularly to build financial resilience and mitigate risks to your business.

Conclusion

Effective financial management and bookkeeping practices are fundamental to the success of your home baking business. By understanding financial principles, implementing accurate bookkeeping practices, developing realistic budgets, employing effective pricing strategies, and managing cash flow proactively, you can strengthen your business's financial health and position it for long-term growth.

In the next chapter, we will explore marketing strategies specifically tailored for promoting your home baking business. Effective marketing is essential for attracting customers, increasing sales, and building brand awareness. Let's continue on this journey to turn your passion into a successful enterprise!

Chapter 11: Marketing Strategies for Your Home Baking Business

Effective marketing is essential for attracting customers, increasing sales, and building brand awareness for your home baking business. In this chapter, we will explore various marketing strategies and tactics to promote your products and connect with your target audience.

Understanding Your Target Audience

Identifying your target audience is the first step in developing effective marketing strategies. Consider the following factors when defining your target audience:

1. **Demographics:** Age, gender, income level, occupation, and family status.
2. **Psychographics:** Lifestyle, interests, values, and buying behaviors.
3. **Geographic Location:** Local community or broader regional/national market.

Understanding your target audience allows you to tailor your marketing messages, product offerings, and promotional strategies to meet their needs and preferences.

Creating a Brand Identity

Developing a strong brand identity sets your home baking business apart from competitors and builds customer loyalty. Consider these elements when creating your brand identity:

1. **Business Name and Logo:** Choose a memorable business name and design a professional logo that reflects your brand's personality and values.
2. **Brand Voice:** Define the tone and style of communication used in your marketing materials and interactions with customers.
3. **Unique Selling Proposition (USP):** Highlight what makes your baked goods unique and why customers should choose your products over others.
4. **Brand Consistency:** Maintain consistency in visual elements, messaging, and customer experience across all marketing channels.

Online Presence and Digital Marketing

Establishing an online presence is crucial for reaching a wider audience and promoting your home baking business. Leverage digital marketing channels and strategies:

1. **Website:** Create a professional website that showcases your products, provides information about your business, and facilitates online ordering. Ensure your website is mobile-friendly and optimized for search engines (SEO) to improve visibility.
2. **Social Media Marketing:** Utilize social media platforms such as Instagram, Facebook, Pinterest, and Twitter to share mouth-watering photos of your baked goods, engage with customers, and promote special offers or new products.
3. **Email Marketing:** Build an email list of customers and prospects interested in your baked goods. Send regular newsletters with updates, promotions, recipes, and baking tips to keep subscribers engaged and encourage repeat purchases.
4. **Content Marketing:** Create valuable content such as blog posts, recipe videos, or baking tutorials that showcase your expertise

and attract potential customers. Share content on your website and social media to educate, entertain, and inspire your audience.

Local Marketing Strategies

Focus on local marketing strategies to establish a strong presence in your community and attract local customers:

1. **Community Events:** Participate in local farmers' markets, food festivals, craft fairs, and community events to showcase and sell your products. Engage with attendees, offer samples, and distribute business cards or flyers.
2. **Collaborations:** Partner with local cafes, restaurants, grocery stores, or businesses to feature your baked goods or create exclusive products. Collaborations can expand your reach and introduce your products to new customers.
3. **Local SEO:** Optimize your online presence for local search by including location-specific keywords in your website content, business listings, and Google My Business profile. Encourage satisfied customers to leave positive reviews to boost local visibility.
4. **Word-of-Mouth Referrals:** Encourage satisfied customers to refer friends and family to your business. Offer incentives such as discounts or free samples for referrals to incentivize word-of-mouth marketing.

Promotional Strategies

Implement promotional strategies to attract customers and drive sales:

1. **Special Offers:** Offer limited-time promotions, discounts for bulk orders, or seasonal specials to incentivize purchases and create urgency.
2. **Loyalty Programs:** Reward repeat customers with a loyalty program that offers discounts, freebies, or exclusive access to new products. Loyalty programs encourage customer retention and increase lifetime value.
3. **Sampling and Tastings:** Provide samples of your baked goods at local events, markets, or in-store demos to allow customers to taste and experience your products firsthand.
4. **Holiday and Seasonal Campaigns:** Create themed promotions or seasonal offerings for holidays such as Valentine's Day, Easter, Thanksgiving, and Christmas. Tailor your products and marketing messages to seasonal trends and customer preferences.

Customer Engagement and Feedback

Engage with customers to build relationships and gather valuable feedback:

1. **Social Media Engagement:** Respond promptly to comments, messages, and reviews on social media platforms. Encourage user-generated content by sharing customer photos or testimonials.
2. **Customer Surveys:** Conduct surveys or feedback forms to gather insights into customer preferences, satisfaction levels, and suggestions for improvement. Use feedback to refine your products and marketing strategies.
3. **Personalized Customer Service:** Provide personalized experiences and exceptional customer service to create positive impressions and foster customer loyalty.

4. **Customer Appreciation:** Show appreciation to loyal customers with personalized thank-you notes, birthday discounts, or exclusive previews of new products.

Monitoring and Measuring Results

Monitor the effectiveness of your marketing strategies and adjust tactics as needed:

1. **Analytics Tools:** Use website analytics, social media insights, and email marketing metrics to track key performance indicators (KPIs) such as website traffic, engagement rates, conversion rates, and return on investment (ROI).
2. **A/B Testing:** Experiment with different marketing approaches, such as ad variations, email subject lines, or promotional offers, to identify what resonates best with your audience.
3. **Feedback Analysis:** Analyze customer feedback, reviews, and survey responses to identify trends, address concerns, and continuously improve your products and services.

Conclusion

Effective marketing strategies are essential for promoting your home baking business, attracting customers, and driving sales. By understanding your target audience, creating a strong brand identity, leveraging digital and local marketing channels, implementing promotional strategies, engaging with customers, and measuring results, you can build awareness, grow your customer base, and achieve long-term success.

Chapter 12: Customer Service Strategies for Your Home Baking Business

Delivering exceptional customer service is fundamental to building strong relationships, generating repeat business, and maintaining a positive reputation for your home baking business. In this chapter, we will explore customer service strategies, best practices, and techniques to exceed customer expectations and foster loyalty.

Understanding the Importance of Customer Service

Customer service encompasses all interactions and experiences that customers have with your business. Positive customer service experiences can:

- **Build Trust and Loyalty:** Establishing trust and fostering loyalty among customers who appreciate your products and the service they receive.
- **Drive Repeat Business:** Encouraging repeat business as satisfied customers return for your delicious baked goods and excellent service.
- **Enhance Reputation:** Building a positive reputation through word-of-mouth recommendations and online reviews from happy customers.

Developing a Customer-Centric Approach

Adopt a customer-centric approach to prioritize the needs and preferences of your customers:

1. **Personalized Communication:** Address customers by name and engage in friendly, personalized interactions both online and in-person.

2. **Active Listening:** Listen attentively to customer inquiries, feedback, and concerns. Demonstrate empathy and understanding to resolve issues effectively.
3. **Timely Responses:** Respond promptly to customer inquiries, messages, and feedback. Use multiple communication channels such as email, phone, and social media to ensure accessibility.
4. **Consistent Service:** Maintain consistency in the quality of your products and service delivery. Strive to exceed customer expectations with every interaction.

Building Relationships with Customers

Establishing meaningful relationships with customers can enhance their overall experience and loyalty to your business:

1. **Follow-Up:** Follow up with customers after purchases to ensure satisfaction and address any concerns or feedback. Express gratitude for their support and feedback.
2. **Customer Feedback:** Encourage customers to provide feedback through surveys, reviews, or testimonials. Use feedback to improve products, service, and overall customer experience.
3. **Personal Touch:** Incorporate personal touches such as handwritten thank-you notes, birthday greetings, or special discounts for loyal customers.
4. **Customer Recognition:** Recognize and appreciate loyal customers through rewards programs, exclusive offers, or early access to new products.

Handling Customer Inquiries and Resolving Issues

Effectively manage customer inquiries, complaints, and issues to maintain customer satisfaction:

1. **Prompt Resolution:** Address customer inquiries and issues promptly and professionally. Provide clear explanations, solutions, or alternatives to resolve concerns.
2. **Empowerment:** Empower frontline staff or yourself to make decisions and take action to resolve customer issues quickly without unnecessary delays.
3. **Positive Communication:** Use positive language and tone in all customer interactions, even when addressing challenges or complaints. Remain calm, courteous, and professional.
4. **Learn from Feedback:** Use customer feedback and complaints as opportunities to identify areas for improvement in products, services, or processes.

Training and Empowering Your Team

If you have a team or plan to hire employees in the future, training and empowering them to deliver excellent customer service is essential:

1. **Training Programs:** Implement customer service training programs to educate employees on best practices, communication skills, and handling customer inquiries and complaints.
2. **Empowerment:** Empower employees to make decisions and take initiative to resolve customer issues independently. Provide guidelines and support to ensure consistency and quality in service delivery.
3. **Feedback and Recognition:** Provide regular feedback and recognition to employees for their efforts in delivering exceptional customer service. Encourage a customer-focused mindset and culture within your team.

Utilizing Technology for Customer Service

Leverage technology to enhance customer service efficiency and accessibility:

1. **Customer Relationship Management (CRM) Systems:** Implement CRM systems to manage customer interactions, track inquiries, and maintain customer profiles and preferences.
2. **Live Chat and Chatbots:** Offer live chat support on your website or utilize chatbots to provide immediate responses to customer inquiries and support requests.
3. **Social Media Monitoring:** Monitor social media platforms for customer comments, mentions, and messages. Respond promptly to engage with customers and address inquiries or concerns publicly.
4. **Email Automation:** Use email automation tools to send personalized messages, order confirmations, and follow-up emails to customers. Segment email lists based on customer preferences and behaviors.

Measuring Customer Satisfaction

Measure and assess customer satisfaction to gauge the effectiveness of your customer service efforts:

1. **Customer Surveys:** Conduct periodic customer satisfaction surveys to gather feedback on overall experience, product quality, service delivery, and areas for improvement.
2. **Net Promoter Score (NPS):** Use NPS surveys to measure customer loyalty and likelihood to recommend your business to others. Analyze NPS scores to identify promoters, detractors, and areas for enhancement.
3. **Online Reviews and Feedback:** Monitor online reviews and testimonials on platforms such as Google, Yelp, and social

media. Encourage satisfied customers to leave positive reviews to build credibility and attract new customers.
4. **Repeat Business and Referrals:** Track repeat business and referrals from satisfied customers as indicators of strong customer relationships and positive word-of-mouth marketing.

Conclusion

Exceptional customer service is a cornerstone of success for your home baking business. By adopting a customer-centric approach, building relationships, resolving issues effectively, training your team, leveraging technology, and measuring customer satisfaction, you can create memorable experiences that delight customers and differentiate your business in a competitive market.

Chapter 13: Growth Strategies for Scaling Your Home Baking Business

Scaling your home baking business involves expanding operations, increasing revenue, and reaching new markets while maintaining quality and customer satisfaction. In this chapter, we will explore growth strategies, expansion opportunities, and considerations for scaling your business effectively.

Assessing Current Business Performance

Before pursuing growth strategies, assess your current business performance and capabilities:

1. **Financial Health:** Review financial statements, cash flow, and profitability to understand your business's financial stability and readiness for growth.
2. **Customer Base:** Evaluate customer demographics, preferences, and feedback to identify opportunities for expanding your customer base and increasing loyalty.
3. **Operational Efficiency:** Assess production capacity, workflow efficiency, and resource utilization to identify areas for improvement and scalability.
4. **Market Analysis:** Conduct market research to identify trends, opportunities, and competitive landscape in the baking industry and target markets.

Expansion Strategies

Explore these growth strategies and expansion opportunities to scale your home baking business:

1. **Increase Production Capacity:**

- **Equipment Investment:** Invest in additional baking equipment, appliances, or technology to increase production capacity and efficiency.
- **Streamline Processes:** Optimize production processes, workflow, and scheduling to maximize output without compromising quality.
- **Staffing:** Hire additional staff or outsource production tasks to meet increased demand and expand operations.

2. **Diversify Product Offerings:**
   - **Expand Menu:** Introduce new baked goods, seasonal specials, or specialty items to attract new customers and encourage repeat purchases.
   - **Customization Options:** Offer customization or personalized baking services for special events, dietary preferences, or corporate orders.
   - **Product Innovation:** Experiment with new recipes, ingredients, or baking techniques to differentiate your offerings and appeal to diverse tastes.

3. **Explore New Markets:**
   - **Local Expansion:** Expand your presence in local markets through partnerships with cafes, restaurants, grocery stores, or specialty food shops.
   - **Online Sales:** Enhance your online presence and e-commerce capabilities to reach customers beyond your local area through shipping or local delivery services.
   - **Wholesale Opportunities:** Pursue wholesale partnerships with retailers, caterers, or businesses to distribute your products to a broader audience.

4. **Marketing and Brand Awareness:**
   - **Digital Marketing:** Increase digital marketing efforts to raise brand awareness, attract new customers, and drive

online sales through social media, email campaigns, and paid advertising.
- **Community Engagement:** Participate in local events, sponsorships, or collaborations to increase visibility, build relationships, and generate word-of-mouth referrals.
- **Customer Loyalty Programs:** Implement loyalty programs, referral incentives, or exclusive offers to reward repeat customers and encourage loyalty.

Financial Planning and Management

Effective financial planning is crucial for supporting business growth and managing financial resources:

1. **Budget Allocation:** Allocate funds strategically for equipment upgrades, marketing initiatives, staff training, and product development to support growth objectives.
2. **Forecasting and Projections:** Develop financial forecasts and projections to anticipate revenue growth, expenses, and funding requirements for expansion initiatives.
3. **Risk Management:** Identify potential risks and challenges associated with growth, such as cash flow fluctuations, increased competition, or supply chain disruptions. Develop contingency plans to mitigate risks and ensure business continuity.
4. **Capital Investment:** Explore financing options such as business loans, grants, or investors to fund expansion projects, equipment purchases, or infrastructure upgrades.

Operational Efficiency and Scalability

Enhance operational efficiency and scalability to support business growth and sustainability:

1. **Systems and Processes:** Implement scalable systems, standard operating procedures (SOPs), and automation tools to streamline operations, reduce costs, and improve productivity.
2. **Inventory Management:** Optimize inventory control and management practices to minimize waste, maintain adequate stock levels, and fulfill customer orders efficiently.
3. **Quality Control:** Maintain stringent quality standards and food safety practices to uphold product integrity, customer satisfaction, and compliance with regulations.
4. **Customer Feedback and Adaptation:** Continuously gather customer feedback, monitor market trends, and adapt business strategies to meet evolving consumer preferences and market demands.

Expansion Considerations

Consider these additional factors when planning for business expansion:

1. **Legal and Regulatory Compliance:** Ensure compliance with local, state, and federal regulations for food safety, licensing, permits, and business operations.
2. **Customer Service Excellence:** Maintain a focus on delivering exceptional customer service as you scale your business to retain loyal customers and attract new ones.
3. **Sustainability Practices:** Incorporate sustainable practices and eco-friendly initiatives into your business operations to appeal to environmentally conscious consumers and enhance brand reputation.

4. **Long-Term Vision:** Develop a clear long-term vision and growth strategy that aligns with your business goals, values, and commitment to quality.

Conclusion

Scaling your home baking business requires careful planning, strategic decision-making, and a commitment to maintaining quality and customer satisfaction. By assessing current performance, exploring growth strategies, enhancing financial management, improving operational efficiency, and considering expansion considerations, you can position your business for sustainable growth and long-term success.

In the next chapter, we will explore management strategies for leading and motivating your team, fostering a positive work environment, and ensuring operational excellence. Effective leadership and team management are essential for driving growth, innovation, and achieving business objectives. Let's continue on this journey to turn your passion into a thriving enterprise!

Chapter 14: Management Strategies for Your Home Baking Business

Effective management is essential for creating a productive work environment, fostering teamwork, and achieving business goals in your home baking venture. In this chapter, we will explore management strategies, leadership principles, and techniques for leading and motivating your team to success.

Setting Leadership Foundations

Establishing strong leadership foundations sets the tone for your business's culture and success:

1. **Vision and Mission:** Define a clear vision and mission statement that outlines your business's purpose, values, and long-term objectives. Communicate these goals to your team to align their efforts and inspire commitment.
2. **Lead by Example:** Demonstrate integrity, passion, and dedication to your business and its values. Lead by example in your work ethic, decision-making, and interactions with customers and team members.
3. **Effective Communication:** Foster open, transparent communication channels to share information, provide feedback, and encourage collaboration among team members. Listen actively to ideas, concerns, and suggestions from your team.
4. **Empowerment:** Empower your team by delegating responsibilities, trusting their abilities, and providing opportunities for professional growth and development. Encourage autonomy and initiative in decision-making within defined parameters.

Building a Positive Work Environment

Creating a positive work environment promotes morale, productivity, and job satisfaction among your team:

1. **Team Culture:** Cultivate a supportive and inclusive team culture that values diversity, respect, and teamwork. Celebrate achievements, milestones, and successes together as a team.
2. **Work-Life Balance:** Support work-life balance by offering flexible schedules, time-off policies, and promoting wellness initiatives to ensure the well-being of your team members.
3. **Training and Development:** Invest in ongoing training, workshops, and skill development programs to enhance the expertise and capabilities of your team. Provide opportunities for cross-training and learning new baking techniques.
4. **Recognition and Rewards:** Recognize and reward team members for their contributions, achievements, and exceptional performance. Implement recognition programs, bonuses, or incentives to motivate and retain talent.

Effective Team Leadership

Develop effective leadership skills to inspire and guide your team towards achieving business objectives:

1. **Goal Setting:** Set clear, achievable goals and milestones for your team that align with business priorities and support overall growth and success. Break down larger goals into smaller, manageable tasks to track progress effectively.
2. **Performance Management:** Establish performance metrics, KPIs, or benchmarks to measure individual and team performance. Provide regular feedback, conduct performance reviews, and offer guidance for improvement.

3. **Conflict Resolution:** Address conflicts or issues among team members promptly and professionally. Foster a collaborative approach to resolving conflicts through mediation, communication, and compromise.
4. **Decision-Making:** Make informed decisions based on data, insights, and input from your team. Involve key stakeholders in decision-making processes to promote transparency and accountability.

Managing Operational Excellence

Ensure operational excellence to maintain quality, efficiency, and consistency in your home baking business:

1. **Quality Control:** Implement rigorous quality control measures to uphold product standards, food safety protocols, and customer satisfaction. Conduct regular inspections and reviews to identify areas for improvement.
2. **Workflow Optimization:** Streamline production processes, workflow efficiency, and scheduling to maximize productivity and minimize waste. Utilize technology, automation, or batch production techniques where applicable.
3. **Inventory Management:** Maintain accurate inventory records, monitor stock levels, and manage ingredient procurement to avoid shortages or excess inventory. Implement inventory tracking systems or software for efficiency.
4. **Customer Service Excellence:** Ensure that customer service standards are upheld by training your team on best practices, responding to customer inquiries promptly, and resolving issues to maintain customer satisfaction.

Adapting to Challenges and Opportunities

Anticipate and adapt to challenges and opportunities in the dynamic baking industry and market environment:

1. **Market Trends:** Stay informed about industry trends, consumer preferences, and competitive developments. Adapt your product offerings, marketing strategies, and business operations accordingly.
2. **Risk Management:** Identify potential risks, such as supply chain disruptions, regulatory changes, or economic downturns. Develop contingency plans and strategies to mitigate risks and ensure business continuity.
3. **Innovation and Creativity:** Foster a culture of innovation and creativity among your team to explore new recipes, products, or packaging solutions. Encourage experimentation and customer feedback to drive continuous improvement.
4. **Sustainability Practices:** Integrate sustainable practices, such as using eco-friendly packaging, sourcing local ingredients, or reducing food waste, into your business operations to appeal to environmentally conscious consumers.

Continuous Improvement and Growth

Embrace a mindset of continuous improvement and growth to evolve and thrive in the competitive baking industry:

1. **Feedback and Reflection:** Solicit feedback from team members, customers, and stakeholders to identify strengths, weaknesses, and areas for enhancement. Reflect on lessons learned and implement actionable insights.
2. **Strategic Planning:** Develop strategic plans and initiatives to guide long-term growth, expansion, and sustainability. Evaluate market opportunities, diversify revenue streams, and invest in future-proofing your business.

3. **Networking and Collaboration:** Build relationships with industry peers, suppliers, and community partners to foster collaboration, share knowledge, and explore collaborative opportunities for mutual benefit.
4. **Celebrating Success:** Celebrate milestones, achievements, and successes with your team to reinforce camaraderie, boost morale, and inspire motivation for future endeavors.

Conclusion

Effective management and leadership are fundamental to the success and growth of your home baking business. By setting strong leadership foundations, fostering a positive work environment, developing effective team leadership skills, ensuring operational excellence, adapting to challenges and opportunities, and embracing continuous improvement, you can cultivate a thriving business that delivers exceptional products and experiences.

In the next chapter, we will explore financial planning strategies for sustaining profitability, managing cash flow, and achieving long-term financial stability in your home baking business. Financial planning is critical for making informed decisions, mitigating risks, and supporting sustainable growth. Let's continue on this journey to turn your passion into a flourishing enterprise!

Chapter 15: Financial Planning Strategies for Your Home Baking Business

Financial planning is crucial for ensuring profitability, managing cash flow, and achieving long-term financial stability in your home baking business. In this chapter, we will explore essential financial strategies, budgeting techniques, and considerations to support your business's growth and success.

Understanding Financial Management

Effective financial management involves overseeing finances, budgeting, forecasting, and making informed decisions to support business objectives:

1. **Financial Statements:** Regularly review financial statements, including income statements, balance sheets, and cash flow statements, to assess profitability, liquidity, and financial health.
2. **Budgeting and Forecasting:** Develop annual budgets and financial forecasts to plan and allocate resources effectively. Monitor actual performance against budgeted goals and adjust plans as needed.
3. **Cash Flow Management:** Manage cash flow by monitoring incoming revenue, outgoing expenses, and maintaining adequate working capital to cover operational costs and investments.
4. **Profitability Analysis:** Analyze profitability by calculating gross profit margins, net profit margins, and assessing the financial performance of individual products or services.

Cost Management and Pricing Strategies

Optimize cost management and pricing strategies to enhance profitability and competitiveness:

1. **Cost Analysis:** Conduct cost analysis to identify and control expenses, including ingredient costs, labor costs, overhead expenses, and operational costs.
2. **Pricing Strategy:** Set competitive pricing based on market trends, competitor pricing, product value, and perceived customer willingness to pay. Consider factors such as ingredient quality, product differentiation, and profit margins.
3. **Value-Based Pricing:** Implement value-based pricing strategies that reflect the quality, uniqueness, and perceived value of your baked goods to justify pricing and maximize profitability.
4. **Promotional Pricing:** Use promotional pricing strategies, such as discounts, bundling, or seasonal offers, to stimulate sales, attract new customers, and manage inventory levels effectively.

Financial Forecasting and Planning

Develop financial forecasts and strategic plans to guide business growth and decision-making:

1. **Revenue Projections:** Estimate future revenue based on historical sales data, market trends, and anticipated customer demand. Consider seasonal variations and economic factors that may impact sales.
2. **Expense Budgeting:** Create detailed expense budgets for operational costs, marketing expenses, ingredient purchases, staffing, and overhead expenses. Monitor expenses closely to control costs and optimize resource allocation.
3. **Capital Investment:** Plan for capital expenditures, such as equipment upgrades, facility expansions, or technology

investments, to support business growth and enhance operational efficiency.
4. **Financial Goals:** Set specific financial goals, such as revenue targets, profit margins, return on investment (ROI), and milestones for achieving sustainable growth and profitability.

Managing Working Capital and Cash Flow

Maintain adequate working capital and manage cash flow effectively to support daily operations and growth initiatives:

1. **Working Capital Management:** Monitor and manage working capital, including accounts receivable, inventory levels, and accounts payable, to ensure liquidity and meet short-term financial obligations.
2. **Cash Flow Forecasting:** Prepare cash flow forecasts to anticipate inflows and outflows of cash, identify potential cash shortages or surpluses, and plan accordingly to maintain financial stability.
3. **Invoice and Payment Policies:** Establish clear invoice and payment policies for customers to ensure timely receipt of payments and minimize accounts receivable aging. Consider offering incentives for early payments or implementing late payment penalties.
4. **Emergency Fund:** Maintain an emergency fund or reserve to cover unexpected expenses, economic downturns, or unforeseen challenges that may impact cash flow or profitability.

Financial Risk Management

Identify and manage financial risks to protect your business and sustain long-term profitability:

1. **Risk Assessment:** Conduct a comprehensive risk assessment to identify potential risks, such as market volatility, supplier disruptions, regulatory changes, or financial instability.
2. **Risk Mitigation Strategies:** Develop risk mitigation strategies, such as diversifying suppliers, securing business insurance coverage, establishing contingency plans, and maintaining strong supplier relationships.
3. **Debt Management:** Manage debt obligations responsibly by monitoring debt levels, interest rates, and repayment schedules. Consider refinancing options, debt consolidation, or negotiating favorable terms with creditors.
4. **Financial Resilience:** Build financial resilience by maintaining a healthy cash flow, minimizing debt, and maintaining adequate liquidity to navigate economic uncertainties and market fluctuations.

Financial Reporting and Accountability

Ensure transparency and accountability in financial reporting and decision-making processes:

1. **Financial Transparency:** Maintain accurate and up-to-date financial records, reports, and documentation to comply with regulatory requirements and facilitate informed decision-making.
2. **Financial Controls:** Implement internal controls and procedures to safeguard assets, prevent fraud, and ensure accuracy in financial reporting. Conduct regular audits or reviews to monitor compliance and identify areas for improvement.
3. **Financial Performance Metrics:** Monitor key financial performance metrics, such as profitability ratios, liquidity ratios, and return on investment (ROI), to evaluate business

performance, track progress towards goals, and make data-driven decisions.
4. **Financial Planning Tools:** Use financial planning tools, software, or accounting systems to streamline financial management processes, automate reporting, and enhance decision-making capabilities.

Conclusion

Effective financial planning and management are essential for sustaining profitability, managing cash flow, and achieving long-term financial stability in your home baking business. By understanding financial principles, implementing budgeting strategies, optimizing cost management, forecasting accurately, managing working capital, mitigating financial risks, and maintaining financial accountability, you can position your business for growth and success.

In the next chapter, we will explore sustainability practices and responsible sourcing strategies for promoting environmental stewardship and ethical business practices in your home baking business. Embracing sustainability can enhance brand reputation, appeal to eco-conscious consumers, and contribute to long-term business sustainability. Let's continue on this journey to turn your passion into a sustainable and thriving enterprise!

Chapter 16: Sustainability Practices for Your Home Baking Business

In today's environmentally conscious marketplace, integrating sustainability practices into your home baking business is not only beneficial for the planet but also enhances brand reputation and attracts eco-conscious consumers. In this chapter, we will explore sustainability initiatives, responsible sourcing strategies, and practical steps to promote environmental stewardship in your operations.

Understanding Sustainability in Baking

Sustainability in baking involves minimizing environmental impact, conserving natural resources, and promoting ethical practices throughout the supply chain:

1. **Environmental Impact:** Assess the environmental footprint of your business operations, including energy consumption, waste generation, water usage, and carbon emissions.
2. **Resource Conservation:** Implement practices to conserve natural resources, such as reducing water usage, optimizing energy efficiency, and minimizing food waste in production and packaging.
3. **Ethical Sourcing:** Source ingredients responsibly from suppliers who adhere to ethical labor practices, fair trade standards, and sustainable farming methods.
4. **Community Engagement:** Engage with the local community, support sustainable agriculture initiatives, and contribute positively to environmental conservation efforts.

Implementing Sustainable Practices

Integrate these sustainable practices into your home baking business operations:

1. **Ingredient Sourcing:**
   - **Local and Seasonal Ingredients:** Prioritize sourcing locally grown or seasonal ingredients to support local farmers, reduce carbon footprint from transportation, and ensure freshness.
   - **Organic and Fair Trade:** Choose organic and fair trade-certified ingredients to promote sustainable farming practices, biodiversity, and fair compensation for farmers.
   - **Sustainable Packaging:** Use eco-friendly packaging materials, such as biodegradable or recyclable packaging, to minimize environmental impact and encourage recycling among customers.
2. **Energy Efficiency:**
   - **Energy Audit:** Conduct an energy audit to identify opportunities for energy savings, such as upgrading to energy-efficient appliances, lighting, and HVAC systems.
   - **Renewable Energy:** Consider investing in renewable energy sources, such as solar panels or wind turbines, to power your baking operations and reduce reliance on fossil fuels.
   - **Energy Conservation:** Implement energy conservation practices, such as turning off equipment when not in use, optimizing baking schedules to reduce idle time, and using energy-efficient cooking methods.
3. **Waste Reduction:**
   - **Composting and Recycling:** Establish composting programs for organic waste, such as leftover ingredients

or food scraps, and implement recycling initiatives for packaging materials, cardboard, and paper.
    - **Food Waste Prevention:** Minimize food waste by accurately forecasting demand, managing inventory effectively, donating surplus food to local charities, and repurposing ingredients creatively.
    - **Reusable Packaging:** Encourage customers to bring their reusable containers or bags for purchasing baked goods to reduce single-use packaging waste.
4. **Water Conservation:**
    - **Water Management:** Implement water-efficient practices, such as installing low-flow faucets and fixtures, repairing leaks promptly, and optimizing water usage during baking and cleaning processes.
    - **Greywater Systems:** Consider implementing greywater systems to reuse water from baking processes for non-potable purposes, such as irrigation or cleaning.
    - **Water Footprint Reduction:** Educate staff on water conservation techniques and encourage mindful water usage throughout your baking operations.

Promoting Environmental Stewardship

Communicate your commitment to sustainability and environmental stewardship to customers, stakeholders, and the community:

1. **Transparency:** Provide transparency about your sustainability practices, ingredient sourcing, and environmental initiatives through your website, packaging labels, and marketing materials.
2. **Educational Outreach:** Educate customers about the benefits of sustainable baking practices, environmental conservation, and

ways they can support sustainability efforts through their purchasing decisions.
3. **Partnerships and Collaboration:** Collaborate with local environmental organizations, community groups, and suppliers committed to sustainability to share knowledge, resources, and support collective efforts.
4. **Certifications and Standards:** Obtain certifications, such as organic, fair trade, or eco-label certifications, to validate your commitment to sustainable practices and differentiate your business in the marketplace.

Measuring Impact and Continuous Improvement

Monitor and evaluate the impact of your sustainability initiatives to drive continuous improvement and demonstrate progress:

1. **Performance Metrics:** Establish key performance indicators (KPIs) to measure energy efficiency, waste reduction, water conservation, and overall environmental impact.
2. **Benchmarking:** Compare your business's sustainability performance against industry benchmarks, standards, or best practices to identify areas for improvement and set goals for future sustainability initiatives.
3. **Stakeholder Engagement:** Engage with stakeholders, including customers, employees, suppliers, and local communities, to gather feedback, share progress on sustainability goals, and foster a culture of environmental responsibility.
4. **Adaptation and Innovation:** Adapt to changing environmental regulations, consumer expectations, and technological advancements by innovating new sustainability solutions and practices for your business.

Conclusion

Integrating sustainability practices into your home baking business is not only a responsible business decision but also a strategic opportunity to attract environmentally conscious consumers, enhance brand reputation, and contribute positively to the planet. By sourcing ingredients responsibly, reducing environmental impact, promoting ethical practices, and engaging with stakeholders, you can build a sustainable business that thrives in a competitive marketplace.

In the next chapter, we will explore marketing strategies and digital presence to promote your home baking business effectively, attract customers, and expand your reach. From social media marketing to creating compelling content, we'll discuss strategies to elevate your brand and drive customer engagement. Let's continue on this journey to turn your passion into a sustainable and successful enterprise!

Chapter 17: Marketing Strategies and Digital Presence for Your Home Baking Business

Marketing is essential for promoting your home baking business, attracting customers, and building a strong brand presence in the marketplace. In this chapter, we will explore effective marketing strategies, digital marketing techniques, and practical steps to elevate your business's visibility and attract your target audience.

Understanding Your Target Audience

Identifying and understanding your target audience is crucial for crafting effective marketing strategies:

1. **Customer Demographics:** Define your ideal customer demographics, including age, gender, income level, location, and lifestyle preferences relevant to your baked goods.
2. **Consumer Behavior:** Analyze consumer behavior, purchasing patterns, and preferences related to bakery products, occasions for purchase, and factors influencing buying decisions.
3. **Market Segmentation:** Segment your target market into distinct groups based on shared characteristics or needs to tailor marketing messages, products, and promotions effectively.
4. **Competitive Analysis:** Conduct a competitive analysis to understand competitors' offerings, pricing strategies, marketing tactics, and unique selling propositions (USPs) to differentiate your business.

Developing Your Marketing Strategy

Craft a comprehensive marketing strategy to reach and engage your target audience effectively:

1. **Brand Identity:** Define your brand identity, including brand values, mission statement, unique selling propositions (USPs), and visual elements (logo, colors, packaging) that resonate with your target audience.
2. **Marketing Objectives:** Set clear, measurable marketing objectives, such as increasing brand awareness, attracting new customers, boosting sales, or expanding market reach, to guide your marketing efforts.
3. **Marketing Mix:** Develop a marketing mix that integrates various channels and tactics, including online and offline strategies, to maximize reach and impact. Consider channels such as social media, website, email marketing, local partnerships, and events.
4. **Budget Allocation:** Allocate a budget for marketing activities, considering costs for advertising, promotions, content creation, graphic design, and any outsourcing or agency fees.

Building Your Digital Presence

Establishing a strong digital presence is essential for modern businesses to connect with customers online:

1. **Professional Website:** Create a professional and user-friendly website that showcases your bakery products, brand story, menu offerings, pricing, contact information, and online ordering options.
2. **Search Engine Optimization (SEO):** Optimize your website and content for search engines to improve visibility in search results. Use relevant keywords, meta tags, and local SEO strategies to attract local customers.
3. **Social Media Marketing:** Leverage social media platforms (such as Instagram, Facebook, Pinterest) to showcase visually appealing images of your baked goods, engage with followers,

share baking tips, promote special offers, and drive traffic to your website.
4. **Content Marketing:** Develop engaging and informative content, such as blog posts, recipes, baking tutorials, customer testimonials, and behind-the-scenes videos, to educate, inspire, and entertain your audience.

Engaging Customers and Building Relationships

Create meaningful connections with customers to foster loyalty and advocacy for your home baking business:

1. **Customer Engagement:** Encourage customer interaction through social media contests, polls, Q&A sessions, and interactive posts that invite feedback, suggestions, and user-generated content.
2. **Email Marketing:** Build an email subscriber list and send regular newsletters, product updates, exclusive offers, and personalized recommendations to stay top-of-mind with customers and drive repeat sales.
3. **Customer Reviews and Testimonials:** Showcase positive customer reviews, testimonials, and user-generated content on your website and social media platforms to build credibility and trust with potential customers.
4. **Customer Loyalty Programs:** Implement customer loyalty programs, referral incentives, birthday discounts, or rewards for repeat purchases to reward loyal customers and encourage repeat business.

Offline Marketing and Local Engagement

Supplement your digital efforts with offline marketing strategies to reach local customers and enhance brand visibility:

1. **Local Partnerships:** Collaborate with local businesses, cafes, restaurants, farmers' markets, or community events to showcase your baked goods, cross-promote offerings, and expand your customer base.
2. **Branding and Packaging:** Design eye-catching packaging that reflects your brand identity and stands out on store shelves or at local events. Use branded merchandise, such as tote bags or stickers, as promotional giveaways.
3. **Event Marketing:** Participate in or sponsor local events, food festivals, charity fundraisers, or pop-up markets to introduce your products to new customers, network with potential clients, and generate buzz around your business.
4. **Print Advertising:** Consider targeted print advertising in local newspapers, magazines, community newsletters, or food guides to reach local residents and highlight your bakery's unique offerings.

Monitoring Performance and Optimization

Monitor the performance of your marketing efforts to measure effectiveness and optimize strategies for continuous improvement:

1. **Analytics and Metrics:** Use analytics tools (Google Analytics, social media insights) to track website traffic, engagement metrics, conversion rates, and ROI from marketing campaigns.
2. **A/B Testing:** Conduct A/B testing for email subject lines, ad creatives, landing pages, and promotional offers to identify high-performing content and optimize marketing campaigns.
3. **Feedback and Adaptation:** Gather feedback from customers, analyze campaign results, and adapt your marketing strategies based on insights and changing market dynamics to stay competitive.

4. **Continuous Learning:** Stay updated on industry trends, digital marketing best practices, and new technologies to innovate and refine your marketing approach for sustained business growth.

Conclusion

Effective marketing strategies and a strong digital presence are essential for promoting your home baking business, attracting customers, and building a loyal customer base. By understanding your target audience, developing a comprehensive marketing strategy, establishing a robust digital presence, engaging customers, fostering local partnerships, and continuously monitoring performance, you can elevate your brand visibility and drive business growth.

In the next chapter, we will explore customer service excellence and best practices for delivering exceptional customer experiences in your home baking business. From personalized service to resolving complaints effectively, we'll discuss strategies to delight customers and build lasting relationships. Let's continue on this journey to turn your passion into a thriving and customer-focused enterprise!

Chapter 18: Customer Service Excellence for Your Home Baking Business

Delivering exceptional customer service is key to building loyalty, fostering positive word-of-mouth, and ensuring repeat business for your home baking venture. In this chapter, we will explore customer service strategies, best practices, and techniques to create memorable experiences that delight your customers.

Understanding Customer Service in Baking

Customer service in baking goes beyond just selling products—it involves creating meaningful interactions and exceeding customer expectations:

1. **Customer-Centric Approach:** Adopt a customer-centric approach by prioritizing the needs, preferences, and satisfaction of your customers in every interaction and transaction.
2. **Personalization:** Tailor your service to meet individual customer preferences, dietary restrictions, special occasions, and personalized requests for baked goods.
3. **Communication Skills:** Develop strong communication skills to listen actively to customer inquiries, provide clear and accurate information about products, and address customer concerns promptly and courteously.
4. **Problem-Solving:** Equip yourself and your team with problem-solving skills to resolve customer issues, handle complaints effectively, and turn negative experiences into positive outcomes.

Building a Customer-Focused Culture

Create a customer-focused culture within your home baking business to prioritize service excellence:

1. **Training and Development:** Provide ongoing training and development opportunities for your team to enhance customer service skills, product knowledge, and interpersonal communication.
2. **Empowerment:** Empower your employees to make decisions and take initiative in resolving customer issues promptly and effectively, within established guidelines.
3. **Feedback Mechanisms:** Implement feedback mechanisms, such as customer surveys, feedback forms, or online reviews, to gather insights, assess satisfaction levels, and identify areas for improvement.
4. **Service Standards:** Define service standards and expectations for your team, including response times, greeting protocols, handling customer inquiries, and maintaining cleanliness and hygiene standards.

Delivering Exceptional Customer Experiences

Strive to create memorable experiences that differentiate your home baking business and build customer loyalty:

1. **Warm Welcomes:** Greet customers warmly, engage in friendly conversation, and create a welcoming atmosphere that makes customers feel valued and appreciated.
2. **Product Knowledge:** Equip your team with comprehensive knowledge about your baked goods, ingredients, preparation methods, and dietary information to assist customers in making informed choices.
3. **Customization and Special Requests:** Accommodate customization requests, special dietary needs, personalized

messages on cakes, and unique orders to exceed customer expectations and create a personalized experience.
4. **Timeliness and Reliability:** Ensure timely fulfillment of customer orders, adhere to promised delivery or pickup times, and maintain consistency in product quality to build trust and reliability.

Handling Customer Inquiries and Resolving Issues

Effectively manage customer inquiries, complaints, and feedback to maintain customer satisfaction and loyalty:

1. **Active Listening:** Listen attentively to customer inquiries, concerns, or feedback without interruption, demonstrating empathy and understanding of their perspective.
2. **Prompt Response:** Respond promptly to customer inquiries via phone, email, social media, or in-person interactions, providing accurate information and solutions to their queries.
3. **Complaint Resolution:** Acknowledge customer complaints with empathy, investigate issues promptly, offer solutions or alternatives, and follow up to ensure customer satisfaction and resolution.
4. **Customer Appreciation:** Express gratitude to customers for their patronage, loyalty, and feedback. Consider sending thank-you notes, offering exclusive discounts, or recognizing loyal customers on social media.

Creating Loyalty Programs and Incentives

Encourage repeat business and reward customer loyalty with incentive programs and special offers:

1. **Loyalty Rewards:** Implement a loyalty program that rewards customers for repeat purchases, referrals, or reaching spending milestones with discounts, freebies, or exclusive access to new products.
2. **Referral Incentives:** Encourage customers to refer friends and family by offering incentives, such as discounts on future purchases or complimentary baked goods for successful referrals.
3. **Personalized Offers:** Send personalized offers, birthday discounts, or anniversary rewards to loyal customers as a token of appreciation for their continued support and patronage.
4. **Feedback and Improvement:** Use customer feedback from loyalty programs to improve service offerings, product quality, and customer experience based on their preferences and suggestions.

Embracing Technology and Convenience

Utilize technology to enhance convenience, accessibility, and customer engagement:

1. **Online Ordering:** Offer online ordering capabilities through your website or mobile app for customers to browse products, place orders, select delivery or pickup options, and make payments seamlessly.
2. **Social Media Engagement:** Use social media platforms to engage with customers, share updates about new products, seasonal promotions, baking tips, and respond to customer inquiries or feedback promptly.
3. **Customer Relationship Management (CRM):** Implement a CRM system to manage customer interactions, track purchase history, preferences, and communication preferences for personalized service.

4. **Digital Marketing:** Leverage digital marketing channels, such as email marketing, social media advertising, and targeted online campaigns, to reach new customers, promote special offers, and drive traffic to your website.

Monitoring and Improving Customer Satisfaction

Continuously monitor customer satisfaction levels and gather insights to enhance service quality and customer experience:

1. **Customer Surveys:** Conduct regular customer surveys or feedback forms to assess satisfaction levels, gather suggestions for improvement, and measure performance against service benchmarks.
2. **Performance Metrics:** Track key performance indicators (KPIs) related to customer service, such as customer retention rates, Net Promoter Score (NPS), average order value, and customer lifetime value (CLV).
3. **Benchmarking:** Benchmark your customer service performance against industry standards, competitor benchmarks, or best practices to identify areas for improvement and set goals for enhancement.
4. **Employee Recognition:** Recognize and celebrate employees who demonstrate outstanding customer service, teamwork, and commitment to exceeding customer expectations.

Conclusion

Exceptional customer service is a cornerstone of success in your home baking business, fostering customer loyalty, positive word-of-mouth referrals, and sustained business growth. By adopting a customer-focused approach, training your team effectively, delivering memorable experiences, resolving issues promptly, creating loyalty programs, embracing technology, and continuously monitoring customer satisfaction, you can build a reputation for excellence and delight customers at every interaction.

In the next chapter, we will explore operational efficiency and productivity strategies for optimizing workflow, managing resources effectively, and ensuring smooth operations in your home baking business. From kitchen organization to inventory management, we'll discuss strategies to enhance efficiency and streamline processes. Let's continue on this journey to turn your passion into a well-oiled baking enterprise!

Chapter 19: Operational Efficiency and Productivity Strategies

Operational efficiency is crucial for optimizing workflow, managing resources effectively, and ensuring smooth operations in your home baking business. In this chapter, we will explore strategies, best practices, and tools to enhance efficiency, streamline processes, and maximize productivity in your baking operations.

Optimizing Kitchen Layout and Organization

A well-organized kitchen layout enhances productivity and efficiency in baking operations:

1. **Workflow Design:** Designate distinct zones for preparation, baking, decorating, packaging, and cleaning to streamline workflow and minimize unnecessary movement.
2. **Workspace Organization:** Organize workstations, storage areas, shelving, and equipment placement for easy access to ingredients, tools, and supplies during baking processes.

3. **Safety and Hygiene:** Maintain cleanliness, sanitation standards, and food safety protocols in compliance with health regulations to ensure a safe working environment for your team.
4. **Equipment Maintenance:** Implement regular maintenance schedules for baking equipment, ovens, mixers, and refrigeration units to prevent breakdowns and ensure optimal performance.

Inventory Management and Ingredient Control

Efficient inventory management and ingredient control are essential for minimizing waste and maintaining supply consistency:

1. **Inventory Tracking:** Use inventory management software or spreadsheets to track ingredient stock levels, monitor expiration dates, and manage reorder points to prevent stockouts.
2. **Just-in-Time (JIT) Inventory:** Adopt JIT inventory practices to minimize storage costs, reduce excess inventory, and ensure fresh ingredients are available for baking production.
3. **Supplier Relationships:** Cultivate strong relationships with reliable suppliers to negotiate favorable terms, secure timely deliveries, and maintain quality standards for ingredients and packaging materials.
4. **Ingredient Standardization:** Standardize recipes, portion sizes, and ingredient measurements to ensure consistency in product quality, taste, and customer satisfaction across batches.

Streamlining Production Processes

Streamline production processes to increase throughput, reduce lead times, and meet customer demand efficiently:

1. **Batch Production:** Implement batch production methods to optimize baking schedules, maximize oven capacity, and reduce idle time between batches.
2. **Production Planning:** Develop weekly or daily production schedules based on demand forecasts, seasonal trends, and special orders to allocate resources effectively and prevent overproduction.
3. **Workflow Automation:** Explore automation tools or technology solutions for repetitive tasks, such as mixing, portioning, or packaging, to improve consistency and productivity in baking operations.
4. **Cross-Training:** Cross-train employees on various tasks and roles within the bakery, including baking, decorating, customer service, and cleaning, to enhance flexibility and resource allocation.

Cost Efficiency and Waste Reduction

Implement cost-saving measures and waste reduction strategies to improve profitability and sustainability:

1. **Cost Analysis:** Conduct regular cost analyses to identify opportunities for cost savings, such as negotiating better pricing with suppliers, optimizing ingredient usage, or reducing overhead expenses.
2. **Waste Management:** Minimize food waste by accurately forecasting demand, repurposing leftover ingredients, donating surplus food to local charities, and implementing composting or recycling programs.
3. **Energy Efficiency:** Invest in energy-efficient equipment, lighting, and appliances to reduce utility costs, lower environmental impact, and optimize energy consumption during baking operations.

4. **Quality Control:** Implement stringent quality control measures to maintain product consistency, freshness, and adherence to food safety standards, minimizing the risk of rework or product wastage.

Staff Training and Development

Invest in ongoing training and development initiatives to enhance skills, knowledge, and performance among your bakery team:

1. **Skills Enhancement:** Provide training on baking techniques, recipe execution, decorating skills, and customer service etiquette to empower employees and ensure high-quality standards.
2. **Team Communication:** Foster open communication, collaboration, and teamwork among staff members to streamline operations, resolve challenges promptly, and achieve collective goals.
3. **Performance Feedback:** Conduct regular performance reviews, provide constructive feedback, recognize achievements, and offer opportunities for career growth and skill development within the bakery.
4. **Employee Morale:** Promote a positive work environment, recognize employee contributions, celebrate milestones, and encourage a sense of pride and ownership in producing exceptional baked goods.

Technology Integration and Digital Tools

Harness technology and digital tools to streamline operations, enhance efficiency, and support business growth:

1. **POS Systems:** Implement a point-of-sale (POS) system to process orders, track sales data, manage inventory levels, and analyze customer purchasing behavior for informed decision-making.
2. **Cloud-Based Solutions:** Utilize cloud-based software for inventory management, financial tracking, scheduling, and remote access to business data from any location.
3. **Online Ordering Platforms:** Offer online ordering and delivery options through your website or mobile app, integrating with your POS system for seamless order processing and customer convenience.
4. **Customer Relationship Management (CRM):** Use CRM software to maintain customer profiles, track interactions, send personalized communications, and nurture customer relationships for repeat business.

Continuous Improvement and Adaptation

Embrace a culture of continuous improvement and adaptability to stay competitive, innovate, and meet evolving customer preferences:

1. **Feedback Loop:** Solicit customer feedback, employee input, and stakeholder insights to identify areas for improvement, innovate new product offerings, and enhance service delivery.
2. **Market Trends:** Stay informed about industry trends, consumer preferences, and competitive developments to capitalize on opportunities, pivot strategies, and adjust business operations accordingly.
3. **Benchmarking:** Benchmark your bakery's performance against industry standards, best practices, or competitors to set goals, measure progress, and strive for operational excellence.
4. **Adaptation to Change:** Anticipate market changes, regulatory requirements, and economic shifts, proactively adapting

business strategies, processes, and resources to maintain resilience and sustainability.

Conclusion

Operational efficiency and productivity are essential for optimizing workflow, managing resources effectively, and achieving sustainable growth in your home baking business. By implementing strategies to streamline production processes, enhance inventory management, control costs, invest in staff training, leverage technology, and foster a culture of continuous improvement, you can enhance operational performance, meet customer expectations, and position your bakery for long-term success.

In the next chapter, we will explore growth strategies and expansion opportunities for scaling your home baking business. From market expansion to diversifying product offerings, we'll discuss strategic approaches to capitalize on opportunities and propel your bakery's growth trajectory. Let's continue on this journey to turn your passion into a thriving and scalable enterprise!

Chapter 20: Growth Strategies and Expansion Opportunities

Growing your home baking business requires strategic planning, market analysis, and leveraging opportunities to expand your customer base and revenue streams. In this chapter, we will explore growth strategies, diversification tactics, and expansion opportunities to scale your bakery operations effectively.

Market Analysis and Opportunity Identification

Conducting a thorough market analysis helps identify growth opportunities, consumer trends, and competitive dynamics in the baking industry:

1. **Market Research:** Gather data on consumer preferences, demographic trends, buying behaviors, and market demand for baked goods in your target geographical area.
2. **Competitive Landscape:** Assess competitors' strengths, weaknesses, pricing strategies, product offerings, and market positioning to identify gaps or opportunities for differentiation.
3. **Customer Insights:** Solicit customer feedback, conduct surveys, and analyze customer behavior to understand preferences, satisfaction levels, and opportunities to expand product offerings or service enhancements.
4. **Trend Identification:** Monitor industry trends, dietary preferences (e.g., gluten-free, vegan), seasonal demand patterns, and emerging consumer preferences for innovation opportunities.

Expansion Strategies for Bakery Operations

Explore strategic approaches to expand your bakery operations and capture new market segments:

1. **Market Segmentation:** Identify and target niche markets or underserved customer segments based on demographics, lifestyle preferences, dietary needs, or special occasions (e.g., weddings, birthdays).
2. **Product Diversification:** Expand your product line to include new categories, flavors, dietary options (e.g., gluten-free, organic), or seasonal specialties to attract a broader customer base and increase sales diversity.
3. **Geographical Expansion:** Consider expanding your reach to new geographical areas through online sales, partnerships with local retailers, farmers' markets, or pop-up locations to reach a wider audience.
4. **Franchising or Licensing:** Explore franchising opportunities or licensing agreements to replicate your bakery concept, brand, and operational model in new locations with lower investment risks.

E-commerce and Online Presence

Harness the power of e-commerce and digital platforms to reach customers beyond your local market:

1. **Online Bakery Shop:** Develop a user-friendly website or e-commerce platform to showcase your products, accept online orders, facilitate payments, and offer delivery or shipping options for customer convenience.
2. **Digital Marketing:** Utilize digital marketing strategies, including social media advertising, search engine optimization (SEO), email marketing campaigns, and content marketing, to drive traffic to your online bakery shop and increase sales.
3. **Customer Engagement:** Leverage social media platforms, blogs, and online forums to engage with customers, share baking tips,

promote seasonal specials, and gather feedback to enhance customer experience.
4. **Customer Data Utilization:** Analyze customer data and online sales metrics to understand purchasing behavior, identify popular products, and tailor marketing efforts to optimize customer acquisition and retention.

Partnerships and Collaborations

Forge strategic partnerships and collaborations to expand distribution channels, enhance brand visibility, and capitalize on synergies:

1. **Retail Partnerships:** Partner with local cafes, restaurants, specialty food stores, or grocery chains to sell your baked goods on consignment or through wholesale agreements, expanding your reach to new customer bases.
2. **Corporate Clients:** Cater to corporate clients, offices, hotels, or event planners by offering customized baked goods, catering services, or corporate gifting solutions for meetings, events, or special occasions.
3. **Collaborative Marketing:** Collaborate with complementary businesses, influencers, food bloggers, or community organizations to co-host events, cross-promote products, or sponsor local initiatives to increase brand awareness and customer engagement.
4. **Supplier Relationships:** Strengthen relationships with suppliers, distributors, and logistics partners to negotiate favorable terms, streamline supply chain operations, and ensure reliable delivery of ingredients and packaging materials.

Financial Planning and Resource Allocation

Develop a comprehensive financial plan and allocate resources effectively to support growth initiatives:

1. **Budget Allocation:** Allocate funds for marketing campaigns, product development, equipment upgrades, staff training, and operational expansions to support strategic growth objectives.
2. **Financial Forecasting:** Conduct financial forecasting and scenario planning to anticipate cash flow needs, revenue projections, profitability targets, and potential financial risks associated with growth initiatives.
3. **Funding Options:** Explore financing options, such as small business loans, lines of credit, grants, or investment partnerships, to secure capital for expansion projects, equipment purchases, or infrastructure upgrades.
4. **Cost Management:** Implement cost-control measures, monitor expenses closely, and seek opportunities to optimize operational efficiencies, reduce overhead costs, and maximize profitability as you scale your bakery operations.

Risk Management and Scalability

Mitigate risks and ensure scalability of your bakery business through strategic planning and operational resilience:

1. **Risk Assessment:** Identify potential risks, market fluctuations, regulatory changes, and operational challenges that may impact business continuity or growth initiatives, developing contingency plans and risk mitigation strategies.
2. **Scalability Planning:** Plan for scalability by evaluating capacity constraints, staffing requirements, production capabilities, and infrastructure needs to accommodate increased demand and expansion into new markets.

3. **Operational Efficiency:** Continuously streamline processes, optimize supply chain management, invest in technology solutions, and enhance workforce capabilities to support scalability and meet growing customer expectations.
4. **Adaptability and Innovation:** Foster a culture of innovation, adaptability, and continuous improvement within your team to respond to market trends, consumer preferences, and competitive dynamics effectively.

Conclusion

Implementing strategic growth strategies, expanding market reach, diversifying product offerings, leveraging digital platforms, forging partnerships, and allocating resources effectively are essential steps for scaling your home baking business successfully. By capitalizing on opportunities, understanding customer needs, optimizing operations, and maintaining financial stability, you can position your bakery for sustainable growth and long-term success in a competitive marketplace.

In the next chapter, we will explore legal considerations, regulatory compliance, and business ethics for your home baking business. From licensing requirements to food safety regulations, we'll discuss essential guidelines to ensure compliance and ethical business practices. Let's continue on this journey to build a resilient and ethically responsible bakery enterprise!

Chapter 21: Legal Considerations, Regulatory Compliance, and Business Ethics

Operating a home baking business involves navigating legal requirements, adhering to food safety regulations, and upholding ethical standards to ensure compliance and build trust with customers. In this chapter, we will explore essential legal considerations, regulatory compliance measures, and ethical practices to guide your business operations.

Understanding Legal Structures and Requirements

Choose the appropriate legal structure and fulfill legal requirements to establish and operate your home baking business legally:

1. **Business Entity Selection:** Select a suitable business structure, such as sole proprietorship, partnership, limited liability company (LLC), or corporation, considering factors like liability protection, tax implications, and operational flexibility.
2. **Business Registration:** Register your business name with the appropriate local, state, or federal authorities, obtain necessary permits or licenses, and comply with zoning regulations or home occupation permits if operating from home.
3. **Tax Obligations:** Obtain an Employer Identification Number (EIN) from the IRS if hiring employees, register for state and local taxes (sales tax, income tax), and maintain accurate financial records for tax reporting purposes.
4. **Insurance Coverage:** Secure business insurance, such as general liability insurance, product liability insurance, or home-based business insurance, to protect against potential risks, accidents, or liability claims related to your baking operations.

Food Safety and Hygiene Standards

Adhere to stringent food safety practices and hygiene standards to ensure the safety and quality of your baked goods:

1. **Regulatory Compliance:** Familiarize yourself with local health department regulations, food handling guidelines, and sanitation requirements applicable to home-based food businesses, including kitchen hygiene, food storage, and temperature control.
2. **Safe Food Handling:** Follow safe food handling practices, including proper handwashing, food preparation techniques, cross-contamination prevention, and allergen management to minimize foodborne illness risks.
3. **Labeling Requirements:** Comply with labeling regulations for packaged food products, including ingredient lists, allergen declarations, nutritional information, and expiration dates to inform consumers and meet legal requirements.
4. **Inspections and Certifications:** Schedule regular inspections by health department officials or third-party auditors to ensure compliance with food safety standards, maintain cleanliness, and address any corrective actions promptly.

Intellectual Property Protection

Protect your intellectual property rights, brand identity, and creative assets associated with your home baking business:

1. **Trademark Registration:** Consider registering trademarks or service marks for your business name, logo, or product branding to prevent unauthorized use and establish exclusive rights to your intellectual property.
2. **Copyright Protection:** Safeguard original recipes, product designs, marketing materials, and website content by asserting

copyright protection, where applicable, to prevent infringement and maintain ownership rights.
3. **Trade Secrets:** Maintain confidentiality and protect proprietary recipes, formulas, or business processes considered trade secrets by implementing confidentiality agreements with employees, suppliers, or business partners.
4. **Legal Disclaimers:** Include legal disclaimers on your website, packaging, or promotional materials to clarify product information, limitations of liability, terms of service, and privacy policies for consumer transparency and legal compliance.

Ethical Business Practices

Adopt ethical business practices and principles to uphold integrity, transparency, and consumer trust in your home baking business:

1. **Customer Transparency:** Provide accurate product descriptions, pricing information, and terms of sale to customers, ensuring transparency in business transactions and building trustworthiness.
2. **Quality Assurance:** Commit to delivering high-quality products, maintaining consistency in taste and appearance, and promptly addressing customer feedback or concerns to uphold reputation and customer satisfaction.
3. **Environmental Responsibility:** Minimize environmental impact by reducing packaging waste, sourcing sustainable ingredients, and implementing eco-friendly practices, such as recycling or composting initiatives.
4. **Fair Employment Practices:** Treat employees with fairness, respect workplace diversity, comply with labor laws regarding wages, working conditions, and employee rights, fostering a positive and inclusive work environment.

Compliance Training and Continuous Improvement

Invest in compliance training, stay informed about regulatory updates, and embrace continuous improvement to enhance business practices:

1. **Staff Training:** Provide ongoing training on food safety protocols, legal compliance requirements, ethical standards, and customer service expectations to empower employees and ensure adherence to best practices.
2. **Regulatory Updates:** Monitor regulatory changes, industry standards, and legal developments affecting home-based food businesses, adapting policies, procedures, and operational practices accordingly.
3. **Internal Audits:** Conduct internal audits or self-assessments to evaluate compliance with legal, regulatory, and ethical standards, identifying areas for improvement, corrective actions, and risk mitigation strategies.
4. **Stakeholder Engagement:** Engage with stakeholders, including suppliers, customers, industry associations, and community partners, to promote ethical practices, social responsibility initiatives, and collaborative solutions.

Conclusion

Navigating legal requirements, ensuring regulatory compliance, and upholding ethical standards are essential aspects of operating a successful and sustainable home baking business. By establishing the right legal structure, prioritizing food safety and hygiene, protecting intellectual property, embracing ethical business practices, and investing in compliance training and continuous improvement, you can build a reputation for reliability, integrity, and consumer confidence.

In the next chapter, we will explore marketing strategies and promotional tactics to attract customers, increase brand visibility, and grow sales for your home baking business. From digital marketing campaigns to local promotions, we'll discuss effective approaches to market your products and reach your target audience. Let's continue on this journey to elevate your bakery's presence and profitability!

Chapter 22: Marketing Strategies and Promotional Tactics

Effective marketing is essential for promoting your home baking business, attracting new customers, and increasing sales. In this chapter, we will explore various marketing strategies, digital tools, and promotional tactics to elevate your brand presence and connect with your target audience effectively.

Developing a Marketing Plan

Create a comprehensive marketing plan to outline goals, target audience, strategies, and tactics for promoting your home baking business:

1. **Target Audience:** Define your target market demographics, preferences, buying behaviors, and consumer needs to tailor marketing messages and promotional efforts effectively.
2. **Unique Selling Proposition (USP):** Identify and communicate your unique selling points, such as premium ingredients, homemade quality, specialty offerings (e.g., gluten-free, vegan), or personalized service, to differentiate your bakery from competitors.
3. **Marketing Goals:** Establish measurable goals, such as increasing online sales, expanding customer base, boosting social media

engagement, or launching new product lines, to guide marketing initiatives and track performance.
4. **Budget Allocation:** Allocate resources for marketing activities, including digital advertising, social media campaigns, promotional events, print materials, and customer incentives, within your budget constraints.

Digital Marketing Strategies

Harness the power of digital marketing channels and online platforms to reach and engage customers effectively:

1. **Website Optimization:** Optimize your website for search engines (SEO) with relevant keywords, compelling content, intuitive navigation, and mobile responsiveness to attract organic traffic and enhance user experience.
2. **Social Media Presence:** Establish a strong presence on social media platforms (e.g., Facebook, Instagram, Pinterest) to showcase visually appealing photos of your baked goods, share baking tips, engage with followers, and promote special offers or seasonal promotions.
3. **Content Marketing:** Create valuable content, such as blog posts, recipe videos, baking tutorials, or customer testimonials, to educate, inspire, and entertain your audience while showcasing your expertise and passion for baking.
4. **Email Marketing Campaigns:** Build an email subscriber list and send regular newsletters, promotional updates, exclusive discounts, or personalized offers to nurture customer relationships, drive sales, and encourage repeat business.

Local Marketing and Community Engagement

Strengthen your brand presence within the local community and cultivate customer loyalty through targeted marketing initiatives:

1. **Local SEO Optimization:** Enhance local search visibility by optimizing Google My Business listing, including business hours, location details, customer reviews, and photos of your bakery, to attract nearby customers searching for baked goods.
2. **Community Events:** Participate in local farmers' markets, food festivals, charity events, or community gatherings to showcase your products, interact with potential customers, and build relationships with community members.
3. **Collaborations and Partnerships:** Collaborate with local businesses, cafes, event planners, or community organizations for cross-promotional opportunities, joint events, or product collaborations to expand brand reach and attract new customers.
4. **Customer Referral Program:** Implement a referral program offering incentives or discounts to customers who refer friends, family, or colleagues to your bakery, leveraging word-of-mouth marketing and increasing customer acquisition.

Promotional Tactics and Customer Incentives

Deploy promotional tactics and customer incentives to stimulate sales, encourage repeat business, and reward customer loyalty:

1. **Special Offers:** Create limited-time promotions, seasonal discounts, bundle deals, or flash sales on popular products to attract price-sensitive customers and drive immediate purchasing decisions.
2. **Loyalty Rewards:** Establish a loyalty program with points-based rewards, exclusive discounts, or freebies for repeat purchases, encouraging customer retention and increasing lifetime value.

3. **Contests and Giveaways:** Host online contests, recipe competitions, or social media giveaways featuring your baked goods as prizes to generate buzz, increase engagement, and expand your social media following.
4. **Personalized Customer Experiences:** Offer personalized services, such as customized cakes, special occasion baking, or personalized packaging with handwritten notes, to enhance customer satisfaction and foster emotional connections.

Monitoring and Measuring Marketing Performance

Monitor and measure the effectiveness of your marketing efforts to optimize strategies, allocate resources wisely, and achieve desired outcomes:

1. **Analytics Tools:** Use web analytics (e.g., Google Analytics) and social media insights to track website traffic, conversion rates, engagement metrics, customer demographics, and sales attribution from marketing campaigns.
2. **ROI Analysis:** Calculate return on investment (ROI) for different marketing channels and campaigns, comparing costs versus revenue generated, to identify high-performing tactics and allocate budget effectively.
3. **Customer Feedback:** Solicit customer feedback through surveys, reviews, or social media interactions to gauge satisfaction levels, identify areas for improvement, and refine marketing strategies based on consumer preferences and insights.
4. **Competitor Benchmarking:** Conduct competitive analysis to benchmark your bakery's marketing performance against industry peers, identify emerging trends, and capitalize on opportunities to differentiate your brand and attract more customers.

Conclusion

Effective marketing strategies and promotional tactics are essential for promoting your home baking business, attracting new customers, and increasing brand visibility in a competitive marketplace. By developing a targeted marketing plan, leveraging digital tools, engaging with the local community, deploying promotional incentives, and measuring marketing performance, you can enhance brand awareness, drive sales growth, and build long-term customer relationships.

In the next chapter, we will explore customer relationship management (CRM) strategies and techniques to nurture customer loyalty, enhance retention rates, and foster advocacy for your home baking business. From personalized communications to customer feedback management, we'll discuss effective CRM practices to maximize customer lifetime value and business success. Let's continue on this journey to cultivate strong relationships and sustain growth for your bakery enterprise!

Chapter 23: Customer Relationship Management (CRM) Strategies

Building strong relationships with customers is crucial for the success and sustainability of your home baking business. In this chapter, we will explore effective CRM strategies, personalized communication tactics, and customer retention techniques to enhance satisfaction, loyalty, and advocacy among your customer base.

Understanding Customer Relationship Management (CRM)

CRM involves strategies and practices for managing interactions with current and potential customers to foster long-term relationships and enhance customer satisfaction:

1. **Customer Segmentation:** Segment your customer base based on demographics, purchasing behavior, preferences, or frequency of orders to tailor marketing messages, promotions, and personalized experiences.
2. **Data Collection:** Gather and analyze customer data, including contact information, purchase history, feedback, and preferences, through CRM software or customer database management to gain insights for targeted marketing efforts.
3. **Personalization:** Customize interactions and communications with customers by addressing them by name, recommending relevant products based on their preferences, and sending personalized offers or birthday greetings to enhance engagement.
4. **Feedback Management:** Solicit customer feedback through surveys, reviews, or direct inquiries to gather insights, address concerns promptly, and continuously improve products, services, and customer experiences.

Effective Communication Strategies

Establish clear and effective communication channels to engage with customers and build rapport:

1. **Multi-channel Approach:** Utilize multiple communication channels, such as email newsletters, social media platforms, website blogs, and direct messaging, to reach customers where they are most active and responsive.
2. **Responsive Customer Service:** Provide prompt and personalized responses to customer inquiries, orders, or feedback through phone calls, emails, live chat support, or social media interactions to demonstrate responsiveness and care.
3. **Educational Content:** Share valuable baking tips, recipe ideas, behind-the-scenes stories, or instructional videos to educate and inspire customers, positioning your bakery as a trusted source of expertise and creativity in baking.
4. **Event Invitations:** Invite loyal customers to exclusive tastings, product launches, baking workshops, or virtual events to foster a sense of community, reward their loyalty, and strengthen relationships beyond transactional interactions.

Customer Loyalty Programs

Implement customer loyalty programs to incentivize repeat purchases and reward loyal patrons:

1. **Points-Based Rewards:** Offer points for every purchase that customers can accumulate and redeem for discounts, free products, or exclusive perks, encouraging frequent visits and increasing customer retention.
2. **Tiered Membership:** Create tiered membership levels (e.g., silver, gold, platinum) with escalating benefits, such as early

access to new products, birthday gifts, or personalized thank-you notes, to motivate higher spending and loyalty.
3. **Referral Incentives:** Reward customers who refer friends or family to your bakery with discounts, free samples, or bonus points, leveraging word-of-mouth marketing and expanding your customer base through trusted recommendations.
4. **Anniversary Rewards:** Celebrate customer milestones, such as anniversary of their first purchase or membership anniversary, with special offers, exclusive discounts, or personalized surprises to reinforce appreciation and strengthen loyalty.

Customer Feedback and Relationship Enhancement

Actively seek and utilize customer feedback to enhance satisfaction, address concerns, and foster continuous improvement:

1. **Feedback Channels:** Provide accessible channels for customers to share feedback, such as feedback forms, online surveys, comment cards, or social media polls, and demonstrate responsiveness by acknowledging and acting on feedback.
2. **Service Recovery:** Handle customer complaints or issues promptly and professionally, offering resolutions, refunds, or replacement products as necessary, to turn negative experiences into positive outcomes and retain customer loyalty.
3. **Relationship Building:** Build genuine connections with customers through personalized interactions, remembering their preferences, celebrating milestones, and showing appreciation for their support to cultivate long-term relationships.
4. **Customer Appreciation:** Express gratitude to loyal customers through personalized thank-you notes, surprise gifts, or exclusive discounts on special occasions, reinforcing their importance to your bakery and fostering emotional bonds.

Measuring Customer Satisfaction and Loyalty

Monitor customer satisfaction levels and measure loyalty metrics to assess the effectiveness of your CRM strategies:

1. **Net Promoter Score (NPS):** Conduct NPS surveys periodically to gauge customer loyalty and likelihood to recommend your bakery to others, using feedback to identify promoters, detractors, and areas for improvement.
2. **Customer Satisfaction (CSAT):** Measure CSAT scores through post-purchase surveys or transactional feedback to evaluate customer satisfaction with products, services, or overall experiences, identifying strengths and areas for enhancement.
3. **Retention Rate:** Track customer retention rates and repeat purchase behavior over time to assess the effectiveness of loyalty programs, customer engagement initiatives, and relationship-building efforts in fostering long-term customer loyalty.
4. **Lifetime Value (LTV):** Calculate LTV to estimate the revenue generated from a customer over their lifetime relationship with your bakery, guiding investment decisions in customer acquisition, retention strategies, and personalized marketing efforts.

Continuous Improvement and Adaptation

Adapt and refine CRM strategies based on customer feedback, market trends, and evolving consumer preferences:

1. **Data Analytics:** Utilize CRM analytics, customer behavior insights, and trend analysis to anticipate customer needs, personalize marketing campaigns, and innovate product offerings that resonate with your target audience.

2. **Competitor Benchmarking:** Benchmark your bakery's CRM practices against industry leaders or competitors to identify best practices, differentiate your brand, and implement innovative strategies that enhance customer engagement and loyalty.
3. **Feedback Integration:** Integrate customer feedback into decision-making processes, operational improvements, and product development initiatives to align business strategies with customer expectations and enhance overall satisfaction.
4. **Adaptive Strategies:** Remain agile and responsive to market changes, technological advancements, and competitive pressures by adapting CRM strategies, embracing new channels, and adopting emerging technologies that enhance customer experiences.

Conclusion

Implementing effective CRM strategies is essential for cultivating strong customer relationships, enhancing satisfaction, fostering loyalty, and driving sustainable growth for your home baking business. By prioritizing personalized communication, deploying customer loyalty programs, soliciting and acting on feedback, measuring satisfaction metrics, and continuously adapting strategies based on insights and trends, you can build a loyal customer base that supports your bakery's success and longevity.

Chapter 24: Operational Resilience and Crisis Management

Maintaining operational resilience and preparedness is essential for navigating challenges, disruptions, and crises that may impact your home baking business. In this chapter, we will explore proactive strategies, contingency planning, and crisis management techniques to safeguard operations, ensure continuity, and protect your bakery's reputation and profitability.

Understanding Operational Resilience

Operational resilience refers to the ability of your bakery business to anticipate, adapt to, and recover from disruptions while maintaining essential functions and delivering consistent service to customers:

1. **Risk Assessment:** Conduct a comprehensive risk assessment to identify potential threats, vulnerabilities, and operational risks that could impact business continuity, such as supply chain disruptions, equipment failures, natural disasters, or public health emergencies.
2. **Business Impact Analysis:** Evaluate the potential impact of identified risks on key business operations, revenue streams, customer service levels, and brand reputation to prioritize risk mitigation efforts and allocate resources effectively.
3. **Contingency Planning:** Develop proactive strategies, contingency plans, and response protocols to mitigate identified risks, minimize operational disruptions, and ensure timely recovery in the event of unforeseen circumstances.
4. **Cross-Functional Collaboration:** Foster collaboration across departments, suppliers, stakeholders, and external partners to enhance communication, coordinate response efforts, and leverage collective expertise in managing operational challenges and crises.

Crisis Management Strategies

Implement effective crisis management strategies to respond promptly, mitigate impacts, and maintain stakeholder confidence during challenging situations:

1. **Crisis Communication Plan:** Establish a crisis communication plan outlining roles, responsibilities, communication channels, and protocols for timely and transparent communication with employees, customers, suppliers, media, and other stakeholders.
2. **Emergency Response Protocols:** Define clear protocols and procedures for handling emergencies, evacuations, product recalls, or safety incidents to ensure the safety of personnel, protect assets, and mitigate potential liabilities.
3. **Business Continuity Planning:** Develop a robust business continuity plan (BCP) with contingency measures, alternate suppliers, redundant systems, and remote work capabilities to sustain essential operations and services during disruptions or crises.
4. **Training and Simulation Exercises:** Conduct regular training sessions, tabletop exercises, or simulations to familiarize employees with crisis response protocols, test the effectiveness of contingency plans, and build organizational readiness for various scenarios.

Supply Chain Management and Vendor Relationships

Enhance supply chain resilience and maintain strong vendor relationships to mitigate risks and ensure continuity of ingredient supply:

1. **Supplier Diversity:** Diversify your supplier base to reduce dependency on single sources and mitigate risks associated with supplier disruptions, quality issues, or fluctuations in raw material availability.
2. **Contractual Agreements:** Establish clear contractual agreements with suppliers, outlining expectations, delivery schedules, quality standards, contingency plans, and dispute resolution mechanisms to ensure reliability and accountability.
3. **Inventory Management:** Maintain adequate inventory levels of essential ingredients, packaging materials, and finished goods to support ongoing production, fulfill customer orders, and buffer against supply chain disruptions or delays.
4. **Risk Monitoring and Mitigation:** Monitor supply chain performance, track key performance indicators (KPIs), and proactively identify potential supply chain risks or vulnerabilities to implement preemptive mitigation strategies and ensure continuity.

Technology Integration and Data Security

Leverage technology solutions and prioritize data security measures to support operational resilience and protect sensitive information:

1. **Technology Adoption:** Invest in scalable technology infrastructure, cloud-based systems, and digital tools for order processing, inventory management, customer relationship management (CRM), and e-commerce operations to enhance agility and efficiency.
2. **Data Backup and Recovery:** Implement robust data backup procedures, encryption protocols, and cybersecurity measures to safeguard customer data, financial records, and operational information from cyber threats, breaches, or data loss incidents.

3. **IT Support and Maintenance:** Maintain regular IT system updates, patches, and maintenance to ensure system reliability, mitigate vulnerabilities, and minimize downtime associated with technical failures or cybersecurity incidents.
4. **Incident Response Planning:** Develop an incident response plan for addressing IT disruptions, cyber attacks, data breaches, or system failures, outlining protocols for containment, investigation, recovery, and communication to mitigate impacts on operations and stakeholders.

Regulatory Compliance and Legal Preparedness

Stay informed about regulatory requirements, compliance obligations, and legal considerations to mitigate legal risks and ensure adherence to industry standards:

1. **Regulatory Monitoring:** Monitor regulatory changes, industry guidelines, and legal developments impacting home-based food businesses, ensuring compliance with food safety regulations, licensing requirements, and health department inspections.
2. **Documentation and Recordkeeping:** Maintain accurate documentation, records of compliance audits, permits, licenses, certifications, and insurance policies to demonstrate regulatory compliance and facilitate audits or inspections as needed.
3. **Legal Counsel:** Consult with legal advisors or regulatory experts to navigate complex legal issues, contractual obligations, liability concerns, and dispute resolution strategies to protect your bakery's legal interests and minimize legal risks.
4. **Insurance Coverage:** Review and update business insurance coverage, including general liability, product liability, business interruption, and cyber insurance policies, to mitigate financial risks associated with operational disruptions, liabilities, or legal claims.

Continuous Improvement and Adaptive Strategies

Embrace a culture of continuous improvement, adaptive strategies, and lessons learned from past experiences to strengthen operational resilience:

1. **Post-Incident Analysis:** Conduct post-incident reviews, root cause analysis, and lessons learned sessions following disruptions or crises to identify areas for improvement, update contingency plans, and enhance preparedness for future challenges.
2. **Scenario Planning:** Develop scenario-based planning exercises or risk scenarios to anticipate potential threats, test response strategies, and enhance organizational readiness for managing various crisis situations effectively.
3. **Stakeholder Engagement:** Engage with stakeholders, including employees, customers, suppliers, and community partners, to communicate resilience efforts, solicit feedback, and foster collaborative solutions in enhancing operational preparedness and crisis management.
4. **Adaptive Leadership:** Demonstrate adaptive leadership qualities, resilience, and decisiveness in navigating uncertainties, making informed decisions, and inspiring confidence among your team and stakeholders during challenging times.

Conclusion

Maintaining operational resilience, implementing proactive crisis management strategies, and prioritizing preparedness are critical for safeguarding your home baking business against disruptions, preserving customer trust, and sustaining long-term success. By conducting risk assessments, developing robust contingency plans, enhancing supply chain resilience, leveraging technology solutions, ensuring regulatory compliance, and fostering a culture of continuous improvement, you can strengthen your bakery's ability to withstand challenges and thrive in a competitive marketplace.

In the next chapter, we will explore innovation in product development, creative recipes, and menu diversification strategies to enhance your bakery's offerings, attract new customers, and differentiate your brand. From seasonal specialties to signature creations, we'll discuss approaches to inspire culinary creativity and meet evolving consumer preferences. Let's continue on this journey to innovate and elevate your bakery's product portfolio!

Chapter 25: Innovation in Product Development and Menu Diversification

Innovation is key to staying competitive and meeting evolving consumer preferences in the home baking business. In this chapter, we will explore strategies for innovating in product development, creating compelling recipes, and diversifying your menu to captivate customers and expand your bakery's appeal.

Understanding Product Innovation

Product innovation involves creating unique, appealing baked goods that resonate with customer tastes, preferences, and dietary trends:

1. **Market Research:** Conduct market research, customer surveys, and trend analysis to identify emerging consumer preferences, flavor trends, dietary considerations (e.g., gluten-free, vegan), and seasonal demands influencing bakery product choices.

2. **Creative Inspiration:** Seek inspiration from culinary trends, global cuisines, seasonal ingredients, cultural celebrations, or local flavors to develop innovative recipes and distinctive baked goods that differentiate your bakery's offerings in the marketplace.
3. **Quality Ingredients:** Source high-quality, fresh ingredients, locally sourced produce, organic options, or specialty ingredients to enhance flavor profiles, nutritional value, and appeal of your bakery products, meeting consumer expectations for quality and authenticity.
4. **Customization Options:** Offer customization options, such as personalized cakes, themed decorations, or bespoke orders, to cater to individual preferences, special occasions, and customer requests, enhancing personalization and customer satisfaction.

Creative Recipe Development

Explore creative recipe development techniques to innovate and elevate your bakery's product portfolio:

1. **Recipe Testing:** Experiment with new flavor combinations, ingredient substitutions, baking techniques, or innovative baking methods to refine recipes, achieve desired taste profiles, and ensure consistency in product quality and presentation.
2. **Seasonal Specialties:** Introduce seasonal specialties, holiday-themed treats, limited-edition flavors, or festive decorations to align with seasonal trends, capitalize on seasonal demand peaks, and create excitement among customers.
3. **Health-Conscious Options:** Develop health-conscious options, such as low-sugar desserts, whole grain baked goods, allergen-friendly recipes, or nutritious snack alternatives, to accommodate dietary preferences and wellness-focused consumer lifestyles.

4. **Signature Creations:** Create signature creations, unique product lines, or flagship items that showcase your bakery's craftsmanship, creativity, and culinary expertise, establishing memorable experiences and customer loyalty.

Menu Diversification Strategies

Diversify your menu offerings to appeal to a broader customer base and cater to diverse tastes and preferences:

1. **Product Variety:** Expand your product range to include a diverse selection of baked goods, including breads, pastries, cakes, cookies, cupcakes, pies, muffins, savory snacks, and specialty items, offering something for every customer occasion and preference.
2. **Seasonal Rotation:** Rotate menu offerings seasonally or periodically to introduce new flavors, ingredients, and menu innovations, keeping customers engaged, encouraging repeat visits, and stimulating curiosity about your bakery's latest offerings.
3. **Menu Bundles and Combos:** Create menu bundles, combo deals, or sampler packs featuring a variety of bakery products, allowing customers to sample different flavors, indulge in assortment trays, or share treats with family and friends.
4. **Cross-Promotional Opportunities:** Collaborate with local businesses, cafes, event planners, or community organizations for cross-promotional opportunities, joint menu features, or co-branded products to expand reach, attract new customers, and foster strategic partnerships.

Marketing and Promotional Strategies

Promote new products, seasonal specialties, and menu innovations effectively to attract customer attention and drive sales:

1. **Product Launch Campaigns:** Plan strategic product launch campaigns, teaser promotions, countdowns, or sneak peeks on social media platforms, website blogs, and email newsletters to generate anticipation and excitement among customers.
2. **Tasting Events and Demos:** Host tasting events, product sampling sessions, or live baking demonstrations in-store, at farmers' markets, or community gatherings to showcase new products, engage with customers, and gather feedback.
3. **Visual Merchandising:** Use visually appealing displays, product photography, and packaging designs that highlight product features, emphasize freshness, convey brand identity, and stimulate impulse purchases among customers.
4. **Customer Feedback and Iteration:** Solicit customer feedback, reviews, and product preferences through surveys, social media polls, or in-store interactions to assess product performance, iterate recipes, and refine menu offerings based on consumer insights and preferences.

Continuous Innovation and Customer Engagement

Maintain a culture of continuous innovation, customer engagement, and responsiveness to evolving consumer preferences:

1. **Feedback Integration:** Integrate customer feedback, reviews, and suggestions into product development processes, recipe refinement, and menu enhancements to align offerings with customer expectations and market trends.
2. **Pilot Programs and Test Markets:** Pilot test new products, menu items, or recipe variations in select locations, online platforms, or focus groups to gauge customer response, gather

performance data, and validate market viability before full-scale rollout.
3. **Collaborative Innovation:** Foster a collaborative approach to innovation by involving employees, pastry chefs, culinary experts, and customer focus groups in brainstorming sessions, ideation workshops, or innovation challenges to inspire creativity and generate new ideas.
4. **Industry Trends and Adaptation:** Stay informed about industry trends, consumer behavior shifts, and competitive landscape changes to anticipate market demands, innovate proactively, and adapt menu offerings and marketing strategies accordingly.

Conclusion

Innovating in product development, creating compelling recipes, and diversifying your menu offerings are key strategies for enhancing your bakery's appeal, attracting new customers, and staying ahead in the competitive home baking market. By focusing on quality ingredients, creative recipe development, menu diversification, effective marketing strategies, and customer engagement initiatives, you can inspire culinary creativity, meet diverse consumer preferences, and cultivate loyalty among your customer base.

Chapter 26: Financial Management and Profitability Analysis

Effective financial management is essential for sustaining profitability, managing expenses, and optimizing financial performance in your home baking business. In this chapter, we will explore strategies for budgeting, cost control, pricing strategies, and profitability analysis to ensure financial health and operational success.

Understanding Financial Management

Financial management involves planning, organizing, controlling, and monitoring financial resources to achieve business objectives, support growth, and maximize profitability:

1. **Budget Development:** Develop a comprehensive budget that outlines projected revenues, expenses, capital investments, and financial goals for your home baking business, providing a roadmap for allocating resources and managing cash flow effectively.
2. **Expense Management:** Implement cost control measures, monitor discretionary spending, negotiate favorable terms with suppliers, and optimize operational efficiency to minimize expenses without compromising product quality or customer satisfaction.
3. **Cash Flow Forecasting:** Forecast cash flow projections, monitor receivables and payables, maintain adequate working capital, and anticipate seasonal fluctuations or financial challenges to ensure liquidity and meet financial obligations on time.
4. **Financial Reporting:** Generate accurate financial statements, balance sheets, income statements, and cash flow reports regularly to track financial performance, assess profitability, and make informed decisions based on financial data and analysis.

Cost Control Strategies

Implement cost control strategies to manage expenses, improve cost efficiency, and enhance profitability margins in your home baking business:

1. **Ingredient Procurement:** Source ingredients in bulk, negotiate volume discounts, explore alternative suppliers, and optimize inventory management practices to reduce raw material costs and maintain product quality standards.
2. **Operational Efficiency:** Streamline production processes, optimize workflow, eliminate waste, and minimize energy consumption to lower production costs, enhance productivity, and improve overall operational efficiency in your bakery.
3. **Labor Management:** Schedule labor efficiently, cross-train staff members, monitor labor costs as a percentage of revenue, and implement performance incentives or productivity metrics to optimize labor utilization and control payroll expenses.
4. **Overhead Expenses:** Review and renegotiate lease agreements, utilities, insurance premiums, and administrative costs to identify opportunities for cost savings, eliminate unnecessary expenditures, and allocate resources more effectively.

Pricing Strategies and Revenue Optimization

Develop strategic pricing strategies to optimize revenue generation, achieve competitive positioning, and maximize profitability for bakery products:

1. **Cost-Plus Pricing:** Calculate product costs, overhead expenses, and desired profit margins to establish competitive yet profitable pricing structures that cover costs and generate adequate returns on investment.

2. **Value-Based Pricing:** Determine customer perceived value, differentiate premium offerings, and justify higher price points based on product quality, uniqueness, artisanal craftsmanship, or personalized customer experiences to capture premium market segments.
3. **Competitive Benchmarking:** Conduct competitive analysis, monitor market trends, and benchmark pricing strategies against industry peers, local competitors, or similar bakery businesses to align pricing decisions with market dynamics and consumer expectations.
4. **Promotional Pricing:** Introduce promotional pricing, seasonal discounts, bundle offers, or loyalty rewards programs to stimulate sales, attract price-sensitive customers, encourage repeat purchases, and drive revenue during promotional periods.

Profitability Analysis and Performance Metrics

Evaluate profitability metrics, analyze financial performance, and measure business success to make informed decisions and drive sustainable growth:

1. **Gross Profit Margin:** Calculate gross profit margins for individual products, product categories, or menu items to assess profitability, identify high-margin products, and prioritize efforts to promote and sell profitable items.
2. **Break-Even Analysis:** Perform break-even analysis to determine the minimum sales volume required to cover fixed costs and achieve profitability, helping to set sales targets, pricing strategies, and operational goals for your bakery business.
3. **Return on Investment (ROI):** Evaluate ROI for capital investments, equipment upgrades, marketing campaigns, or product innovations to assess profitability, allocate resources

effectively, and prioritize initiatives that deliver the highest return on investment.
4. **Key Performance Indicators (KPIs):** Monitor key financial indicators, such as revenue growth, profit margins, average order value, customer acquisition costs, and inventory turnover rates, to track business performance, identify trends, and facilitate data-driven decision-making.

Financial Planning and Investment Strategies

Develop long-term financial planning strategies, reinvest profits, and explore investment opportunities to support business growth and sustainability:

1. **Capital Budgeting:** Evaluate investment opportunities in equipment upgrades, facility expansions, technology investments, or new product development initiatives based on projected returns, strategic alignment, and risk assessment criteria.
2. **Emergency Fund:** Establish an emergency fund or contingency reserve to mitigate financial risks, address unexpected expenses, or navigate economic downturns without compromising day-to-day operations or long-term growth objectives.
3. **Debt Management:** Manage debt responsibly, maintain favorable credit terms, and consider refinancing options to reduce interest costs, improve cash flow, and optimize capital structure for your bakery's financial health and stability.
4. **Savings and Investment Strategies:** Set aside funds for future growth initiatives, retirement planning, or personal financial goals, leveraging tax-efficient savings vehicles, investment diversification, or wealth management strategies to build financial resilience and wealth over time.

Conclusion

Effective financial management, including budgeting, cost control, pricing strategies, and profitability analysis, is essential for optimizing financial performance, sustaining profitability, and achieving long-term success in your home baking business. By prioritizing financial transparency, operational efficiency, strategic pricing decisions, and performance monitoring, you can strengthen financial resilience, capitalize on growth opportunities, and navigate challenges with confidence.

In the next chapter, we will explore marketing strategies, branding initiatives, and customer acquisition techniques to promote your bakery, enhance brand visibility, and attract new customers. From digital marketing campaigns to community engagement efforts, we'll discuss approaches to build brand equity and expand your bakery's reach in the marketplace. Let's continue on this journey to elevate your bakery's brand presence and customer engagement!

Chapter 27: Marketing Strategies and Branding Initiatives

Effective marketing and branding are crucial for promoting your bakery, attracting new customers, and building a loyal customer base. In this chapter, we will explore strategies for marketing your products, enhancing brand visibility, and implementing customer acquisition techniques to drive business growth.

Developing a Marketing Strategy

A well-defined marketing strategy outlines your bakery's goals, target audience, positioning, and tactics to achieve competitive advantage and market success:

1. **Market Segmentation:** Identify target market segments based on demographics, psychographics, consumer behaviors, and purchasing preferences to tailor marketing efforts and messaging effectively to specific customer groups.
2. **Brand Positioning:** Define your bakery's unique value proposition, brand promise, and competitive differentiation to establish a distinctive brand identity that resonates with target customers and sets your bakery apart from competitors.
3. **Marketing Channels:** Select appropriate marketing channels, such as social media platforms, website blogs, email newsletters, local advertising, community events, or influencer partnerships, to reach target audiences, amplify brand messages, and drive customer engagement.
4. **Integrated Campaigns:** Develop integrated marketing campaigns, seasonal promotions, cross-channel marketing initiatives, or co-branded partnerships that align with brand objectives, enhance brand visibility, and generate buzz around new product launches or special offers.

Digital Marketing Strategies

Leverage digital marketing strategies to enhance online presence, engage with customers, and drive traffic to your bakery's website or physical location:

1. **Social Media Marketing:** Utilize social media platforms, such as Facebook, Instagram, Pinterest, and Twitter, to showcase visually appealing product photos, share baking tips, promote special offers, interact with followers, and cultivate a community of loyal customers.
2. **Content Marketing:** Create valuable, informative content, including recipe blogs, baking tutorials, behind-the-scenes videos, customer testimonials, or chef's tips, to establish thought leadership, educate your audience, and drive organic traffic to your website.
3. **Search Engine Optimization (SEO):** Optimize your website content, product descriptions, blog posts, and landing pages with relevant keywords, meta tags, and local SEO strategies to improve search engine rankings, attract organic traffic, and increase visibility among local customers searching for bakery products.
4. **Email Marketing Campaigns:** Launch targeted email marketing campaigns, personalized newsletters, product updates, or exclusive promotions to nurture customer relationships, encourage repeat purchases, and drive sales conversions through effective email segmentation and automation.

Local Marketing and Community Engagement

Engage with the local community, establish relationships with nearby businesses, and participate in community events to build brand loyalty and attract local customers:

1. **Local Partnerships:** Collaborate with local cafes, restaurants, farmers' markets, or event organizers for joint promotions, cross-promotional opportunities, or co-hosted events that increase brand exposure and attract new customers from complementary businesses.
2. **Community Sponsorships:** Sponsor local charity events, school fundraisers, sports teams, or cultural festivals to demonstrate corporate social responsibility, support community initiatives, and strengthen brand affinity among local residents.
3. **In-Store Events:** Host in-store events, baking workshops, product tastings, or seasonal celebrations that encourage customer engagement, showcase new products, and provide memorable experiences that drive foot traffic and increase sales.
4. **Customer Loyalty Programs:** Implement customer loyalty programs, reward incentives, referral bonuses, or VIP discounts to incentivize repeat business, foster customer loyalty, and turn satisfied customers into brand advocates who promote your bakery through word-of-mouth recommendations.

Brand Identity and Visual Branding

Develop a cohesive brand identity, including logo design, brand colors, packaging aesthetics, and visual branding elements that convey your bakery's unique personality and appeal to target customers:

1. **Logo and Brand Design:** Design a distinctive logo that reflects your bakery's values, craftsmanship, and product offerings, ensuring brand consistency across marketing materials, signage, packaging, and digital platforms.
2. **Packaging and Presentation:** Create visually appealing packaging designs, branded boxes, labels, or eco-friendly packaging options that enhance product appeal, communicate

quality, and differentiate your bakery's products on retail shelves or during customer deliveries.

3. **Brand Storytelling:** Share your bakery's origin story, founder's journey, culinary inspirations, or artisanal baking techniques through storytelling narratives, blog posts, social media content, or customer interactions that resonate emotionally with your audience and strengthen brand authenticity.
4. **Customer Feedback and Reputation Management:** Monitor online reviews, customer feedback, and social media mentions to respond promptly, address customer inquiries or concerns, and cultivate a positive brand reputation built on trust, transparency, and exceptional customer service.

Measuring Marketing Effectiveness

Evaluate marketing campaign performance, track key performance indicators (KPIs), and analyze return on investment (ROI) to optimize marketing strategies and achieve measurable business results:

1. **Performance Metrics:** Measure KPIs, such as website traffic, social media engagement, email open rates, conversion rates, customer acquisition costs (CAC), and lifetime value (LTV) to assess marketing effectiveness, identify top-performing channels, and allocate resources efficiently.
2. **A/B Testing:** Conduct A/B tests, split testing, or multivariate experiments on marketing campaigns, ad creatives, landing pages, or promotional offers to identify winning variations, optimize campaign performance, and enhance customer response rates.
3. **Customer Analytics:** Utilize customer analytics tools, CRM software, or marketing automation platforms to capture customer data, analyze purchasing behaviors, segment

customer personas, and personalize marketing communications for targeted audience segments.
4. **Continuous Improvement:** Iterate marketing strategies based on data-driven insights, customer feedback, and market trends to refine messaging, optimize campaign tactics, and sustain long-term growth in brand awareness, customer acquisition, and revenue generation.

Conclusion

Implementing effective marketing strategies, branding initiatives, and customer acquisition techniques is essential for promoting your bakery, expanding brand visibility, and attracting new customers in a competitive marketplace. By leveraging digital marketing channels, engaging with the local community, developing a distinctive brand identity, and measuring marketing effectiveness, you can build brand equity, foster customer loyalty, and achieve sustainable business growth.

In the next chapter, we will explore customer service excellence, personalized customer experiences, and retention strategies to enhance customer satisfaction, drive repeat business, and build long-term relationships with your bakery's clientele. Let's continue on this journey to deliver exceptional service and cultivate loyal customers who become advocates for your bakery!

Chapter 28: Customer Service Excellence and Retention Strategies

Exceptional customer service and personalized experiences are key to building customer loyalty, driving repeat business, and fostering a positive reputation for your home baking business. In this chapter, we will explore strategies to deliver outstanding customer service, personalize customer interactions, and implement retention strategies that ensure long-term success.

Delivering Exceptional Customer Service

Providing exceptional customer service involves anticipating customer needs, exceeding expectations, and creating memorable experiences that leave a lasting impression:

1. **Customer-Centric Approach:** Adopt a customer-centric approach, prioritizing customer satisfaction, listening to feedback, and tailoring services to meet individual needs, preferences, and expectations, fostering a customer-focused culture within your bakery.
2. **Training and Empowerment:** Train your team on customer service best practices, effective communication, conflict resolution, and problem-solving skills to ensure they are well-equipped to handle customer inquiries, complaints, and special requests professionally and efficiently.
3. **Prompt Response:** Respond promptly to customer inquiries, emails, phone calls, and social media messages, demonstrating responsiveness, attentiveness, and a commitment to addressing customer concerns in a timely manner.
4. **Personalized Interactions:** Personalize customer interactions by addressing customers by name, remembering their preferences, and tailoring recommendations or offers based on their past

purchases and feedback, creating a sense of individualized attention and care.

Creating Memorable Customer Experiences

Enhancing customer experiences involves creating memorable moments, delightful surprises, and thoughtful touches that resonate with customers and foster loyalty:

1. **Ambiance and Atmosphere:** Create a warm, inviting ambiance in your bakery, with pleasant décor, comfortable seating, and a welcoming atmosphere that encourages customers to relax, enjoy their treats, and feel valued as guests.
2. **Product Presentation:** Pay attention to product presentation, ensuring that baked goods are beautifully displayed, packaging is attractive, and every item is presented with care and attention to detail, enhancing the overall customer experience.
3. **Special Touches:** Introduce special touches, such as complimentary samples, personalized thank-you notes, birthday discounts, or surprise treats for loyal customers, to create delightful moments that surprise and delight your clientele.
4. **Customer Appreciation Events:** Host customer appreciation events, loyalty program member gatherings, or exclusive tastings to show gratitude to your loyal customers, foster community, and create opportunities for face-to-face interactions and relationship building.

Implementing Customer Retention Strategies

Retaining customers involves implementing strategies that encourage repeat business, build loyalty, and create long-term relationships with your clientele:

1. **Loyalty Programs:** Develop a loyalty program that rewards repeat purchases, offers exclusive discounts, and provides incentives for referrals, encouraging customers to return frequently and spread the word about your bakery.
2. **Consistent Quality:** Maintain consistent product quality, freshness, and taste across all bakery offerings, ensuring that customers have a positive and reliable experience every time they visit, reinforcing trust and satisfaction.
3. **Customer Feedback Loop:** Establish a feedback loop by regularly soliciting customer feedback through surveys, suggestion boxes, or online reviews, and actively incorporating their suggestions into your products, services, and operations to show that their opinions are valued and impactful.
4. **Proactive Communication:** Keep customers informed about new product launches, seasonal specials, upcoming events, and bakery news through regular communication channels, such as email newsletters, social media updates, or personalized messages, fostering ongoing engagement and connection.

Handling Customer Complaints and Issues

Effectively managing customer complaints and resolving issues promptly is crucial for maintaining customer trust and loyalty:

1. **Active Listening:** Listen actively to customer complaints, acknowledge their concerns, and empathize with their experiences, demonstrating that you value their feedback and are committed to resolving their issues.
2. **Prompt Resolution:** Address customer complaints and issues promptly, offering solutions, replacements, or refunds as necessary, and ensuring that customers feel heard, respected, and satisfied with the resolution.

3. **Follow-Up:** Follow up with customers after resolving their complaints to ensure their satisfaction, thank them for their feedback, and invite them to share their thoughts on their overall experience, reinforcing your commitment to exceptional service.
4. **Continuous Improvement:** Use customer complaints and feedback as opportunities for continuous improvement, identifying areas for enhancement in your products, services, or processes, and implementing changes that prevent future issues and elevate the overall customer experience.

Building a Customer-Centric Culture

Fostering a customer-centric culture within your bakery involves aligning your team, values, and practices around a shared commitment to exceptional customer service and satisfaction:

1. **Team Alignment:** Ensure that all team members understand and embrace the importance of customer service excellence, providing training, resources, and support to empower them to deliver outstanding service consistently.
2. **Values and Mission:** Define and communicate your bakery's core values and mission, emphasizing a commitment to customer satisfaction, quality, and community, and encouraging your team to embody these values in their daily interactions and responsibilities.
3. **Recognition and Rewards:** Recognize and reward team members who demonstrate exceptional customer service, positive attitudes, and proactive problem-solving, reinforcing the importance of customer-centric behavior and motivating others to follow suit.
4. **Customer-Centric Practices:** Implement customer-centric practices, such as regular team meetings to discuss customer

feedback, collaborative problem-solving sessions, and initiatives that prioritize customer needs and enhance their overall experience with your bakery.

Conclusion

Delivering exceptional customer service, creating personalized customer experiences, and implementing effective retention strategies are essential for building customer loyalty, driving repeat business, and fostering a positive reputation for your home baking business. By adopting a customer-centric approach, enhancing customer interactions, and prioritizing customer satisfaction, you can cultivate long-term relationships, enhance brand loyalty, and achieve sustained business success.

In the next chapter, we will explore legal considerations, compliance requirements, and risk management strategies for your home baking business. From understanding licensing and permits to implementing safety protocols, we'll discuss approaches to ensure regulatory compliance and mitigate potential risks. Let's continue on this journey to secure your bakery's legal foundation and operational resilience!

Chapter 29: Legal Considerations and Risk Management

Ensuring legal compliance and effective risk management is crucial for the sustainability and protection of your home baking business. In this chapter, we will explore the essential legal requirements, compliance obligations, and risk management strategies to safeguard your business operations and mitigate potential liabilities.

Understanding Legal Requirements

Complying with legal requirements is fundamental to operating your home baking business ethically and within the boundaries of the law:

1. **Business Licensing:** Obtain the necessary business licenses and permits required to operate a home baking business in your local jurisdiction. This may include a general business license, food handling permit, and home kitchen certification.
2. **Zoning Regulations:** Ensure your home baking business complies with local zoning laws and residential ordinances. Verify that your neighborhood permits commercial activities and home-based businesses.
3. **Health and Safety Standards:** Adhere to health and safety regulations set by local health departments. This includes proper food storage, hygiene practices, kitchen sanitation, and compliance with health inspections.
4. **Labeling and Packaging Laws:** Follow labeling and packaging regulations, including ingredient lists, allergen information, nutritional facts, and expiration dates, to ensure transparency and consumer safety.

Navigating Compliance Obligations

Maintaining compliance with various regulations and industry standards is critical for legal and operational integrity:

1. **Food Safety Certification:** Obtain food safety certification, such as ServSafe or similar programs, to demonstrate your knowledge of safe food handling practices and commitment to food safety.
2. **Tax Compliance:** Register for a tax identification number, maintain accurate financial records, and comply with local, state, and federal tax obligations, including sales tax collection and reporting requirements.
3. **Employment Laws:** If you hire employees, comply with labor laws, including minimum wage requirements, workers' compensation insurance, employee classification, and workplace safety regulations.
4. **Intellectual Property Protection:** Protect your intellectual property, such as your business name, logo, and proprietary recipes, by registering trademarks or copyrights as necessary to safeguard your brand identity.

Implementing Risk Management Strategies

Risk management involves identifying, assessing, and mitigating potential risks to ensure business continuity and minimize liabilities:

1. **Liability Insurance:** Obtain general liability insurance, product liability insurance, and home-based business insurance to protect against potential claims, accidents, or damages related to your bakery operations.
2. **Food Safety Protocols:** Implement stringent food safety protocols, including regular kitchen inspections, proper food storage, temperature control, and staff training, to prevent foodborne illnesses and contamination risks.

3. **Emergency Preparedness:** Develop an emergency preparedness plan, including fire safety measures, evacuation procedures, first aid kits, and emergency contact information, to ensure the safety and well-being of your team and customers.
4. **Data Security:** Protect customer data and payment information by implementing secure payment processing systems, data encryption, and privacy policies to prevent data breaches and ensure compliance with data protection regulations.

Navigating Legal Disputes and Challenges

Understanding how to navigate legal disputes and challenges is essential for protecting your business interests and resolving conflicts effectively:

1. **Contract Management:** Draft clear, legally binding contracts for suppliers, vendors, employees, and partners to outline expectations, responsibilities, and terms of agreements, reducing the risk of misunderstandings or disputes.
2. **Dispute Resolution:** Establish dispute resolution procedures, including mediation or arbitration clauses, to address conflicts or disagreements amicably and avoid costly litigation.
3. **Legal Counsel:** Consult with legal professionals or business attorneys to seek advice on complex legal matters, contract reviews, compliance issues, or potential legal challenges to ensure informed decision-making and legal protection.
4. **Document Retention:** Maintain thorough records of business transactions, contracts, communications, and compliance documentation to provide evidence and support in case of legal inquiries or disputes.

Ethical Considerations and Social Responsibility

Operating your home baking business ethically and responsibly fosters trust, goodwill, and positive community relationships:

1. **Ethical Sourcing:** Source ingredients ethically, prioritizing local suppliers, fair trade products, and sustainable practices that support environmental sustainability and social responsibility.
2. **Community Engagement:** Engage with the local community through charitable donations, volunteer activities, or sponsorships, demonstrating your commitment to giving back and fostering community well-being.
3. **Transparent Practices:** Maintain transparency in your business practices, from ingredient sourcing to pricing and product labeling, ensuring honesty and integrity in all customer interactions and business operations.
4. **Customer Education:** Educate customers about your business practices, product ingredients, and safety measures through informative content, workshops, or tours, enhancing customer trust and loyalty.

Conclusion

Navigating legal considerations, compliance requirements, and risk management strategies is essential for the sustainability and protection of your home baking business. By understanding and adhering to legal obligations, implementing effective risk management practices, and operating ethically, you can safeguard your business operations, minimize liabilities, and build a strong foundation for long-term success.

In the final chapter, we will explore the importance of continuous improvement, innovation, and growth strategies to ensure the ongoing success and evolution of your home baking business. From expanding product lines to exploring new markets, we'll discuss approaches to keep your bakery thriving and adaptable in a dynamic marketplace. Let's continue on this journey to sustain and grow your bakery's success!

Chapter 30: Continuous Improvement, Innovation, and Growth Strategies

The sustainability and growth of your home baking business depend on your ability to continuously improve, innovate, and adapt to changing market conditions. In this chapter, we will explore strategies to foster continuous improvement, drive innovation, and implement growth strategies that keep your bakery thriving and adaptable in a dynamic marketplace.

Fostering a Culture of Continuous Improvement

Continuous improvement involves regularly assessing and enhancing your business processes, products, and services to achieve higher efficiency, quality, and customer satisfaction:

1. **Regular Reviews:** Conduct regular reviews of your business operations, financial performance, customer feedback, and market trends to identify areas for improvement and implement necessary changes.
2. **Employee Involvement:** Encourage employee involvement in the continuous improvement process by seeking their input, suggestions, and insights on ways to enhance efficiency, product quality, and customer service.
3. **Process Optimization:** Streamline your business processes, from inventory management to production workflows, to reduce

waste, minimize errors, and improve overall operational efficiency.
4. **Quality Control:** Implement robust quality control measures to ensure consistency in product quality, taste, and presentation, addressing any deviations promptly to maintain high standards.

Driving Innovation in Your Bakery

Innovation is key to staying competitive and meeting evolving customer demands. Embrace creativity and experimentation to introduce new products, services, and experiences:

1. **New Product Development:** Continuously develop and test new recipes, flavors, and product offerings based on customer preferences, seasonal trends, and culinary innovations to keep your menu fresh and exciting.
2. **Customer-Centric Innovation:** Involve customers in the innovation process by soliciting their ideas, conducting taste tests, and gathering feedback on potential new products or service enhancements.
3. **Technology Adoption:** Leverage technology to streamline operations, enhance customer experiences, and improve efficiency. This could include adopting bakery management software, online ordering systems, or digital marketing tools.
4. **Creative Marketing:** Experiment with creative marketing campaigns, such as themed product launches, interactive social media contests, or collaborations with influencers, to generate buzz and attract new customers.

Implementing Growth Strategies

Growth strategies are essential for expanding your business, reaching new markets, and increasing revenue streams. Consider the following approaches to drive business growth:

1. **Market Expansion:** Explore opportunities to expand your market reach by targeting new customer segments, entering new geographic areas, or offering delivery services to broaden your customer base.
2. **Product Diversification:** Diversify your product portfolio by introducing complementary products, such as beverages, savory items, or baking kits, to attract a wider audience and increase sales.
3. **Partnerships and Collaborations:** Form strategic partnerships and collaborations with other businesses, such as cafes, restaurants, or local retailers, to co-promote products, cross-sell offerings, and enhance brand visibility.
4. **Franchising and Licensing:** Consider franchising your bakery concept or licensing your brand to other entrepreneurs, allowing you to expand your business footprint without directly managing additional locations.

Investing in Marketing and Brand Building

Effective marketing and brand building are crucial for attracting and retaining customers, enhancing brand awareness, and driving business growth:

1. **Brand Consistency:** Maintain consistent branding across all customer touchpoints, including your website, social media, packaging, and in-store experience, to reinforce brand identity and recognition.
2. **Content Marketing:** Create engaging and valuable content, such as blog posts, videos, and social media updates, that showcases

your expertise, shares your brand story, and connects with your audience on a personal level.
3. **Customer Engagement:** Foster ongoing customer engagement through loyalty programs, email marketing, social media interactions, and personalized communications that nurture relationships and encourage repeat business.
4. **Public Relations:** Leverage public relations efforts, such as press releases, media coverage, and influencer partnerships, to increase your bakery's visibility, build credibility, and attract new customers.

Enhancing Customer Experiences

Delivering exceptional customer experiences is vital for building loyalty, driving word-of-mouth referrals, and differentiating your bakery in a competitive market:

1. **Personalized Service:** Personalize customer interactions by remembering their preferences, offering tailored recommendations, and providing a warm, welcoming environment that makes them feel valued.
2. **Customer Feedback:** Actively seek and act on customer feedback to identify areas for improvement, address concerns, and continuously enhance the customer experience.
3. **Special Events and Promotions:** Host special events, workshops, and promotions that create memorable experiences for customers, such as baking classes, seasonal celebrations, or exclusive product launches.
4. **Customer Support:** Provide excellent customer support by being responsive, attentive, and proactive in addressing customer inquiries, issues, and special requests, ensuring a positive experience at every touchpoint.

Planning for Future Growth

Strategic planning and goal setting are essential for guiding your bakery's future growth and ensuring long-term success:

1. **Business Plan Review:** Regularly review and update your business plan to reflect new goals, market opportunities, and strategic initiatives that align with your vision for growth.
2. **Financial Planning:** Implement sound financial planning and budgeting practices to manage cash flow, allocate resources effectively, and invest in growth initiatives that drive profitability.
3. **Scalability:** Assess the scalability of your business model, identifying areas where you can replicate successful processes, expand production capacity, and accommodate increased demand without compromising quality.
4. **Innovation Roadmap:** Develop an innovation roadmap that outlines your plans for new product development, market expansion, technology adoption, and other growth initiatives, ensuring a proactive approach to business evolution.

Conclusion

Continuous improvement, innovation, and strategic growth are vital for the ongoing success and evolution of your home baking business. By fostering a culture of continuous improvement, embracing innovation, implementing growth strategies, investing in marketing, enhancing customer experiences, and planning for future growth, you can ensure your bakery remains competitive, adaptable, and poised for long-term success.

Congratulations on completing this journey through the essential aspects of starting and growing a successful home baking business. May your passion for baking, commitment to excellence, and entrepreneurial spirit drive your bakery to new heights, delighting customers and creating lasting memories with every delicious bite.

www.ingramcontent.com/pod-product-compliance
Lightning Source LLC
Chambersburg PA
CBHW071922210526
45479CB00002B/522